RESEARCH HIGHLIGHTS IN SOCIAL WORK 29

Developing Services for Older People and Their Families

Research Highlights in Social Work

Planning and Costing Community Care
Edited by Chris Clark and Irvine Lapsley
ISBN 1 85302 267 5
Research Highlights in Social Work Series 27

Performance Review and Quality in Social Care
Edited by Anne Connor and Stewart Black
ISBN 1 85302 017 6
Research Highlights in Social Work Series 20

Developments in Short-Term Care
Breaks and Opportunities
Edited by Kirsten Stalker
ISBN 1 85302 134 2
Research Highlights in Social Work Series 25

Social Work
Disabled People and Disabling Environments
Edited by Michael Oliver
ISBN 1 85302 178 X pb
ISBN 1 85302 042 7 hb
Research Highlights in Social Work Series 21

Poverty, Deprivation and Social Work
Edited by Ralph Davidson and Angus Erskine
ISBN 1 85302 043 5
Research Highlights in Social Work Series 22

Social Work and the European Community
Edited by Malcolm Hill
ISBN 1 85302 091 5
Research Highlights in Social Work Series 23

RESEARCH HIGHLIGHTS IN SOCIAL WORK 29

Developing Services for Older People and Their Families

Edited by Rosemary Bland

Jessica Kingsley Publishers
London and Bristol, Pennsylvania

First published in the United Kingdom in 1996 by
Jessica Kingsley Publishers Ltd
116 Pentonville Road
London N1 9JB, England
and
1900 Frost Road, Suite 101
Bristol, PA 19007, U S A

Copyright © 1996 Robert Gordon University,
Research Highlights Advisory Group, School of Applied Social Studies

© Table 2.1, 2.2 and 2.3 Crown copyright

Library of Congress Cataloging in Publication Data
A CIP catalogue record for this book is available from the Library of Congress

British Library Cataloguing in Publication Data
Developing services for older people and their families. -
(Research highlights in social work ; 29)
1. Aged - Services for - Great Britain 2. Family services -
Great Britain.
1. Series II. Bland, Rosemary
362.6'0941

ISBN 1-85302-290-X

Printed and Bound in Great Britain by
Athenaeum Press, Gateshead, Tyne and Wear

Contents

Part III: The Practice Context

Introduction and Overview

Rosemary Bland

The change of focus in old age research and social work practice

The first Research Highlights edition devoted to findings about older people's needs and the effectiveness of social work services for them was published in 1982. Since that time, the focus of research interest in ageing has broadened from a preoccupation with residential care to evaluations of services and innovations which support frail older people in their own homes, reflecting the change of focus in social work practice. Other studies which illustrate how the vast majority of older people in the population who are not social work services users manage and resolve the difficulties which confront them as they age, provide us with knowledge about the strengths and weaknesses of informal networks, and what services which aim to support or substitute for family care when needed (see e.g. Wenger 1984, Qureshi and Walker 1989) must be able to offer if they are to be effective. The statutory obligation of social work and social services departments towards older people has been to promote their welfare and to provide residential care for those who needed it. Thirteen years on from the first volume, there have been changes in legislation but other aspects of older people's social situation have not changed.

Under the NHS and Community Care Act 1990, social work and social services authorities now have a duty to assess the social care needs of frail older people and are expected to arrange services to meet these assessed needs, where feasible within a community context, and with finite resources. This has resulted in social workers becoming involved with many more older people, the majority of whom wish to remain at home despite, in some cases, having needs which are complex and sometimes difficult to meet in a domiciliary setting. Despite the anxieties which exist over the ability of authorities to deliver a level and quality of community care that is affordable and supportive to users, there is little doubt that this legislation has been instrumental in getting the needs of older people and their families who support them more firmly onto the social work agenda than ever before.

However, this change of emphasis from residential to community care in social work has been accompanied by reductions in acute and long stay provision for older people by the National Health Service. This has put considerable pressure on local authorities, not least on their residential and nursing home budgets. There is, therefore, both a financial as well as an ideological imperative for the community care reforms in general and for care management in particular, to succeed.

The heterogeneity of older people

It has not proved possible to address in one volume, all the different facets of life in old age which should inform social work practice. Older people are, like the rest of us, a very heterogeneous group and as a result, their needs and how they wish these to be met are also very diverse. This is true also for older people from black and ethnic minorities, for whom the experience of ageing in a second homeland may not be a very positive one. The need to forge partnerships with different community groups in order to develop services which are culturally and socially acceptable and appropriate to older people in these groups is now being recognised.

There are also particular issues for social workers regarding the way in which older people with sensory disabilities have their care needs assessed, and how they are enabled to use services which maximise their autonomy and independence. Old age being predominantly a female experience, as is that of being a carer, there is now a growing body of research which has explored the extent to which the reality of the centrality of women as users, carers and service providers around old age is acknowledged by policymakers and managers, and reflected in the nature of services and how they are allocated.

Although two chapters in this volume discuss research into the effectiveness of specific services as they meet the needs of people with dementia, there is such a growing body of research into the optimal ways of meeting the needs of those older (and younger) people who develop the disease that they are the subject of a separate, sister volume.

Innovations in residential care options for older people are another area which deserve a volume to themselves. This edition of Research Highlights concentrates deliberately on the community care context within which social work with older people takes place, and examines the ways in which the legislative aims of multi-agency collaboration and a user and carer-led approach to needs assessment and care practice are becoming a reality.

The Community Care legislation was only fully implemented in April 1993, so experience of implementing the reforms is still very recent and varied. Nevertheless, there is a body of knowledge which can usefully analyse the difficulties and barriers which need to be overcome as well as report on initiatives and strategies which are worth emulating.

The welcome and growing interest in older people among social workers indicates that this area of practice is less unpopular than it was in the seventies and eighties (see Stevenson and Parsloe 1978, Howe 1980, Phillipson 1982). Negative attitudes to old age are shared by other professional groups such as doctors and nurses (Maclean 1989) and reflect one of the main obstacles to the development of good practice and high quality services which have to be overcome.

The social context of social work with older people

In order to put the research findings into context, the first section of the book addresses a number of key issues which affect current social work practice with older people. In the first chapter, Chris Phillipson and Neil Thompson discuss the ways in which the negative perceptions about old age are socially constructed and reinforced. They identify potentially destructive policies and practices such as infantilisation and dehumanisation and suggest that a partnership model of social work with older people can avoid such tendencies, stressing the importance of incorporating an anti-ageist perspective into both social work theory and practice. In his chapter on the demography of ageing, Tony Warnes shows that it is decreases in infant mortality and infertility which have brought about the growth in the proportion of older people in the population. He uses the way that this growth has been reported, analysed and discussed, to make the case for a more measured and positive approach to the challenge of supporting older people who need help from the Health and other services whose greater availability have contributed to their survival. What people can expect to enjoy in life as they grow older is influenced by their health and by their income. In her chapter on the financial circumstances of older people, Christina Victor demonstrates that inequities in life chances and employment income are continued into old age, with women, people living alone and those over the age of 75 being the groups most likely to experience increasing poverty as a part of their experience. So the financial circumstances of a large proportion of older people are not improving and look unlikely to do so. The final chapter in Part I is Alan Walker's review of social policy and practice trends among EC states. He identifies the widespread switch from a residential to a community care-based model of provision for older people, brought about by political and economic forces rather than the grass roots influence of service users. His somewhat gloomy conclusion that there will be only minimal improvements in care services available to older EC citizens is balanced by the hope that the growing political confidence of older people's organisations in Europe to demand better services may yet bring about a new agenda based on users' rights, rather than the discretion of providers.

The implications of moving to user and carer-centred practice

In Part II, the book examines how social work is addressing the community care needs of older people within a multi-disciplinary and multi-agency context, looking first at the role that housing has to play in influencing the quality of community care. Bridget Franklin analyses the various housing-based options that are now available to people in old age, weighing up their advantages and their limitations. Emphasising the significance of dwelling as 'home' to the older person and the implications this has for moving, she urges a more person-centred approach to the issue and stresses the importance of social work agencies involving housing professionals more closely in the planning and delivery of community care. This need to focus on the service user is explored by Fiona Myers and Charlotte MacDonald in their chapter on the experience of users and carers being able to exercise choice following needs assessments. Drawing on an evaluation of community care implementation in four Scottish regions, they conclude that although practitioners were in favour of greater consumer involvement in defining and meeting needs, aspects of practice and structural constraints sometimes made this a variable reality. Interviews with users and carers revealed potential and actual conflicts of interest over the choice of service options available to them. The authors conclude that, ultimately, user choice is restricted by professional definitions of need and eligibility.

When considering the needs of people with dementia and those of their family members who are caring for them, there is often a conflict of interest between the two groups. Julie Curran's paper on the development of day care services for people with dementia discusses research findings about the potential of day care to be a positive and beneficial experience for the older person, as well as providing essential relief from the caring task for their relatives. So far, there is more evidence about the benefit to carers than to people with dementia, although some carers comment positively about the benefits they observe in the older person. The finding that accessing day care several days a week may involve the person with dementia attending two or three different settings highlights the current fragmentation of the service. Enid Levin and Jo Moriarty's paper examines their research findings about respite care for older people with dementia and their caring relatives. Given that the older people in their sample were a very frail and highly dependent group, they were surprised to find that nearly three quarters of survivors were still being cared for at home a year later. Although carers valued the caring breaks greatly, the research highlighted the need for services to be more intensive and flexible in what they offer, since the survival of the older person at home is reliant on the continuity of their family carer being able and willing to continue their support.

Although 'informal carers' have now established themselves as a group with needs which require to be addressed, this is not necessarily true of the people who live with the older person they support, particularly spouses and siblings. Gillian Parker examines research findings about the circumstances of people who are same generation carers to show that some of our assumptions about this group are mistaken. While service providers may believe that the intimacy of a married relationship means that spouses can give help with personal care more easily than other relatives, some of them find it extremely difficult and others may find that their emotional closeness makes the role of caring for a partner with severe physical or mental frailty extremely stressful. There may be a tendency for spouses to 'protect' the vulnerable partner by refusing help from friends and from services, leading to 'role over-load' and the possibility of crises. Sibling carers are an even less well-studied group and the proportion who co-reside with their brother or sister seems to be declining. The amount of support that is provided by services to spouse and sibling carers has tended to be small and has been getting smaller. Gillian Parker suggests that while profes-sionals must focus on supporting people who live alone and who have no family carers, there are signs that spouses and siblings may not always be seen by service providers as carers. This is serious because they are heavily involved in caring roles and, by virtue of their age, are the most vulnerable group of carers.

Developments in social work practice with older people: the evidence so far

In Part III we look at the context within which social workers and care managers are working with older people. Brian Hardy and colleagues report on a recently completed evaluation of a pilot care management project in Durham, located in three GP fundholding practices. The evaluation compared the assessment and care management process for people over the age of 75 who were helped by the General Practice care managers, with that for people receiving the newly developing main-stream assessment and care management service, by means of case studies. Although these arrangements are still very new, the authors report that users, carers and professionals were all agreed that the full-time co-location of care managers with GPs was very popular. The scheme resulted in active co-operation between social work and medi-cal and nursing colleagues, appropriate, timely and responsive serv-ices, and eroded the unhelpful stereotyping by professionals and the mutual suspicion which had existed previously. Alison Petch's exami-nation of the progress of the implementation and development of care management so far in Scotland draws on research interviews with sixty-five care managers in four regions; two where the 'role' model of practice has been adopted and two where it is seen as a 'task'. The research found a general criticism by care managers and care co-ordi-nators of their training for this new activity: either of its quality or the lack of any training at all. Practitioners varied in the extent to which they had access to budgets to purchase services for users and how these budgets could or could not be spent. The introduction of IT systems had not yet been the success that was hoped and care managers felt uncertain about the parameters within which they were operating. The chapter concludes that implementing such major changes in the way people are provided with support and services was always going to take time. Additional factors such as local government reorganisation and changes in NHS services to older people will also affect the speed of progress. The message is that we must be patient.

One area of debate in social work over a long period has been the relative merits of genericism versus specialisation in terms of individual and team workload. Since the recent legislation, there has been an even greater move towards individual and team specialisms, either organised around distinct client groupings such as older people, people with mental health difficulties or with a learning disability, or as community care or adult care teams, covering all adult groups. The research which Roger Fuller and Emmanuelle Tulle-Winton report on was carried out just before the Community Care Act came into force. Their study explored whether the perceived advantages of having specialist teams had a measurable effect on the assessment of need and service delivery to older people. The research was conducted in area teams in Scotland and the North of England, looking at specialist 'elderly' teams, Community Social Work-oriented generic teams and three, what the researchers called 'hybrid', teams where individual social workers specialised informally in work with a particular client group. Specialist teams produced more elaborate assessments than the others, identified a wider range of problems, liaised more with other agencies and identified greater needs among carers, particularly with re-referrals. Specialist teams also differed in what they offered, providing significantly more support services outside the home than other teams. However, retrospective interviews with users and carers did not reveal significant differences in expressed satisfaction or dissatisfaction with services received which could be attributed solely to team type. The highest rates of dissatisfaction were, not surprisingly, articulated by younger, disabled adults. Whether specialist teams can deliver a superior quality of service to users in the current community care context is a matter for further enquiry. The positive findings about their assessment and liaison skills allow for a degree of optimism.

Much of this volume has been concerned with research findings about the changes which have come about in social work and social services in recent times. Olive Stevenson examines how far changes in practice have progressed since the community care reforms and finds that the evidence is mixed. Whether the relationship between older people and the professionals who work with them will become more or less equal she finds hard to predict. While arguing for the urgent need for social workers to take an empowering stance in their work with older people, Olive Stevenson points out that for some very vulnerable older people, social workers have a responsibility to provide support and protection. Empowerment which results in abrogation of responsibility, or neglect of older people who need help from social workers is a travesty. Safeguarding and enabling such autonomy as they are able to exercise should be the hallmark of good practice.

Signposts for the future

To sum up, this volume begins and ends with challenges to the social work profession about its attitudes towards work with older people. As part of an ageist as well as an ageing society, there is a role for social workers in working towards the elimination of this kind of oppression in the same way that they have challenged racism, sexism and disablism to which some older people may also be vulnerable. This is a tall order, for we have also shown that expectations of social workers are rising, both from users and carers and from policymakers. Opinions about the ability of the community care reforms to deliver better support and care vary; it could go either way. The main conclusions seem to be that:

- the potential of older people to influence policies and services to support later life has not yet been realised;
- social workers need to adopt an empowering and anti-ageist approach to their work with older people;
- day care and respite services are too fragmented; they need to be more intensive and more flexible. There is research evidence about their benefit to carers but not about their effects on users;
- family carers are crucial to older people remaining at home: the most vulnerable, namely spouses and siblings, are not always recognised as carers;
- inter-professional and inter-agency collaboration is helped by co-location and by specialist teams;

- care managers are uncertain about the parameters within which they are operating, particularly in the use of budgets; their training and technological support require attention;
- older people and their family carers feel that their choices about services are restricted.

While resources are unlikely ever to keep up with appropriately rising expectations, it is attitudes and, above all, social workers' ability to think and act creatively in partnership with older people and their families in meeting needs that will make the vital difference.

References

Howe, D. (1980) 'Divisions of labour in the area teams of social services departments.' *Social Policy and Administration* 14, 2, 133–50.

Maclean, U. (1989) *Dependent Territories: the Frail Elderly and Community Care*. Nuffield Provincial Hospitals Trust.

Phillipson, C. (1982) *Capitalism and the Construction of Old Age*. London: Macmillan.

Qureshi, H. and Walker, A. (1989) *The Caring Relationship: Elderly People and their Families*. Basingstoke: Macmillan.

Stevenson, O. and Parsloe, P. (1978) *Social Services Teams: the Practitioner's View*. London: HMSO.

Wenger, C. (1984) *The Supportive Network*, London: Allen and Unwin.

Part I

The Social Context

Chapter 1

The Social Construction of Old Age
New Perspectives on the Theory and Practice of Social Work with Older People

Chris Phillipson and Neil Thompson

Introduction

The impact of an ageing population has caused considerable debate and discussion over the past few years. These discussions have emerged against a background of rapid change in terms of the context of ageing. Three important features may be identified here: first, the growth in public awareness and interest in ageing issues – these sharpened by concerns over the ability of governments to provide financial security for future generations of pensioners (Phillipson 1991, Bengston and Achenbaum 1993). Second, in the case of Britain, the impact of legislation in the field of community care and the movement towards a mixed economy of care (Phillipson 1994). Third, the growth in early retirement and the evolving concept of 'the third age', this raising issues about changes in policies and attitudes to realise the full potential of later life (Midwinter 1992).

This social context of ageing has itself influenced debates within the field of social gerontology. In particular, in the 1980s an important theoretical debate emerged focusing on the social construction of old age. The themes associated with this perspective highlighted the extent to which the wider social and political environment influenced the lives of older people. This was analysed in terms of areas such as the production of poverty in old age (Walker 1993), in the development of ageism (Bytheway 1994); and the experience of marginalisation within the family and residential homes (Biggs 1993, Kingston and Penhale 1995).

In assessing the value of the social construction approach, this chapter will first, review some of the key arguments arising from this perspective; second, consider some implications for social work practice with older people; third, review some emerging issues in the study and experience of old age.

The social construction of later life

The social construction perspective was developed by a number of researchers during the late 1970s and early 1980s. The model grew out of the politicisation of issues surrounding old age, together with the problems faced by traditional theories in developing an effective response to the unfolding crisis in public expenditure. Early studies using this perspective included: *The Aging Enterprise* by Carroll Estes (1979); 'The Structured Dependency of the Elderly' by Peter Townsend (1981); 'Towards a Political Economy of Old Age' by Alan Walker (1981); Chris Phillipson (1982); *Political Economy, Health and Aging* by Estes, Gerard, Zones and Swan (1984); *Old Age in the Welfare State by John Myles* (1984), and *Ageing and Social Policy* by Chris Phillipson and Alan Walker (1986).

A general review of the arguments adopted has been brought together in a collection edited by Minkler and Estes (1991) entitled *Critical Perspectives on Aging*. Later studies influenced by this approach include those by Bernard and Meade (1993), Biggs (1993), Arber and Ginn (1991), Hugman (1994) and Biggs, Phillipson and Kingston (1995).

A major concern of these studies has been to challenge a view of growing old as a period dominated by physical and mental decline (the biomedical model of ageing). This model was attacked for its association of age with disease, as well as for the way that it individualised and medicalised the ageing process. The approach taken by what may be termed critical gerontology is a view that old age is a social rather than a biologically constructed status. In the light of this, many of the experiences affecting older people can be seen as a product of a particular division of labour and structure of inequality, rather than a natural part of the ageing process. Alan Walker (1980) elaborated this perspective with his concept of the 'social creation of dependency' in old age, and Peter Townsend (1981) used a similar term when he described the 'structured dependency' of older people. This dependency was seen to be the consequence of the forced exclusion of older people from work, the experience of poverty, institutionalisation and restricted domestic and community roles.

The paradigm developed by critical gerontology is shared by developments in the study of other age groups. For example, many of the themes in the collection of essays edited by James and Prout (1991) *Constructing and Reconstructing Childhood*, explore issues debated in social gerontology in the 1980s. The connections between age groups have been further explored by Hockey and James (1993) in *Growing Up and Growing Old*. A central theme of this study is the extent to which power is lost and gained at different points through the life course, and the possibility of both young and older people being affected by processes of infantilisation (see further below).

In respect of social construction or critical gerontology, the main themes of this approach have been concerned with:

- Challenging a form of biological reductionism, whereby the real physiological and biological changes which take place with ageing are often used as a justification for denying old people the right to participate in decisions which affect their lives.

- Showing that age must be seen in relation to the individual's location within the social structure, including factors such as: race, class, gender, and the type of work (paid and unpaid) performed by an individual through his or her life.

- Demonstrating that later life is a time of reconstruction, with older people active in the search for meaning – through work, leisure and intimate friendships.

- That the lives of older people may be seen to be in tension with the nature of capitalism as an economic and social system, with the poverty of older people, their exclusion from work and their image as a burden on society, illustrating this relationship.

The above arguments will now be assessed as regards their implications for social work with older people, with particular emphasis on the issue of the kind of discrimination experienced by older people in later life.

Ageism and older people

The social construction model has certainly been fruitful in terms of the analysis of ageing at macro-economic and macro-social levels. At the same time, a particular form of oppression identified from the way older age was constructed was identified in the form of ageism. First coined by Robert Butler (1963), the concept increased in popularity with the growth of such social movements as the Grey Panthers in the US (Kuhn, 1977). Ageism is defined, according to Butler (1987, p.22):

> 'As a process of systematic stereotyping and discrimination against people because they are old, just as racism and sexism accomplish this for skin colour and gender...Ageism allows the younger generation to see older people as different from themselves: thus, they suddenly cease to identify with their elders as human beings and thereby reduce their own fear and dread of ageing... At times ageism becomes an expedient method by which society promotes viewpoints about the aged in order to relieve itself from responsibility towards them.'

Biggs (1993) notes that ageism is now established as a starting point for investigations into older age. Although a number of criticisms have been made of this concept (Kogan 1979, Bytheway 1994), it has been valuable in providing connections with the activities of institutions on the one side, and beliefs about old age on the other. Ageism finds institutionalised expression through job discrimination, loss of status, stereotyping and dehumanisation. It focuses on the way in which old age is transformed from a gain and extension of the life course, into an economic and social problem or burden. At the same time, it also opens out the possibility of links with different forms of professional practice with older people. To assess how these might be developed, the next section of this chapter considers the implication of an anti-ageist perspective for social work practitioners.

Developing anti-ageist practice

The development of anti-ageist practice involves addressing a range of important issues that influence, constrain or facilitate good practice. These factors can be seen to apply at four levels: social work practice at the individual level; influencing and shaping the practice of other social workers; influencing policy and agency procedures; and theory development. This section will address each of these in turn, with a view to moving towards an understanding of anti-ageist practice.

Patterns of individual practice

Traditional practice with older people relies heavily on assumptions that, on closer critical scrutiny, reveal themselves to be reflections of ageist ideology. A basic component of anti-ageist practice, therefore, is a willingness to subject our own practice to critical review – a preparedness to reconsider established patterns of practice. Such a review can be addressed in terms of a number of key concepts, namely: empowerment, partnership, and challenging destructive processes such as infantilisation and dehumanisation. We shall consider each of these in turn.

Empowerment refers to the process of helping people increase the degree of control they have over their lives. It involves:

- *challenging stereotypes of dependency.* A focus on empowerment seeks to ensure that older people are not made dependent on workers or services. The concept of 'interdependency' (Phillipson 1989) is a useful one insofar as it acknowledges that older people have not only needs but also positive strengths to offer.

- *giving people choices.* Instead of acting as the 'expert' who has all the answers, a more appropriate approach is one in which we help to identify choices, and support the older person through the process of deciding upon options and carrying them through.

- *focusing on self-esteem.* The negative stereotypes of ageism tend to be internalised by older people. This internalised oppression can then have a detrimental effect on confidence and self-esteem (Thompson 1995). Empowerment can counter the potential negative effects of ageism on self-worth.

- *recognising oppression.* Traditional approaches can be criticised for failing to recognise the significance of oppression. For example, in working with ethnic minorities, a common misunderstanding is that it is better to 'treat everyone the same' (the 'colour-blind' approach). This fails to demonstrate sensitivity to people's ethnic needs, values and patterns, and the experience of racism (Blakemore and Boneham 1993). Similarly, it needs to be recognised that older people constitute an oppressed group as a result of the predominance of ageism. If this point is not acknowledged, practice may reinforce ageist stereotypes.

This last point is particularly significant for, as Ward and Mullender (1993) argue, we need to guard against traditional practice being translated into a new language without fundamental change to how service users are treated: so what does it mean to empower someone? It has become clear that, by itself, the term cannot provide an adequate foundation for practice. The language of empowerment trips too lightly off the tongue and is too easily used merely as a synonym for 'enabling' (Mitchell 1989, p.148). Unless it is accompanied by a commitment to challenging and combatting injustice and oppression, which shows itself in actions as well as words, this professional Newspeak allows anyone to rewrite accounts of their practice without fundamentally changing the way it is experienced by service users.

Partnership, as a practice principle, is closely linked to empowerment insofar as it entails the worker using his or her power, influence and access to resources to work alongside service users in pursuing jointly agreed goals. This involves encouraging older people to play as full and active a part as possible in the process of assessing needs and developing an action plan geared towards meeting them. It is a movement away from a medical model of service delivery in which the problem is 'diagnosed' by the expert and a course of 'treatment' prescribed. The partnership model, by contrast, locates the worker's expertise in facilitating the joint identification of needs to be met, problems to be solved and barriers to be overcome. In this way, worker and service user can collaborate in forging a way forward that has a far higher likelihood of success than an approach involving externally defined needs and an externally imposed means of meeting them.

A skilful approach to partnership can bring many benefits, not least the following:

- a higher degree of participation by the service user that can have a positive effect on confidence and self-esteem – a greater feeling of control over what is happening;

- a broader picture of the circumstances, incorporating the service user's perspective as well as the worker's;

- less resistance to necessary changes as a result of a higher degree of commitment to the joint process.

Smale *et al.* (1993, p.11) draw a distinction between a 'Questioning' approach to assessment and care management and an 'Exchange' approach. The former presents the worker as someone who forms a professional judgement on the basis of asking a number of questions. This process therefore tends to be dominated by the worker's agenda. The latter, by contrast, involves an exchange of information through which needs and potential solutions are jointly explored:

> 'In the Exchange model two or more people come together and arrive at a mutual understanding of the nature of the problem, its solution or management, through the interaction between them. Typically the professional will not lead the content of the dialogue because he or she will not know any more, if as much, as the other people about the situation, its problems, or what existing resources could contribute to the "solution", *i.e.* the potential components of a "package of care". The professional follows or tracks what the other people say and communicate. To lead is to assume that the professional knows where to go, and often this will be straight to a service-led response.'

The Exchange model illustrates working in partnership, and helps to clarify what is involved in replacing unsatisfactory traditional models of practice with an approach premised on anti-ageism.

A further important aspect of anti-ageism is a preparedness to counter destructive processes. We shall focus on two in particular, namely infantilisation and dehumanisation. Infantilisation refers to the tendency to treat older people as if they were children. This involves patronising them, not consulting them and generally disregarding their rights as adult citizens (Thompson 1992). Hockey and James (1993) describe the ways in which metaphors of childhood are used to shape the experience of ageing and, in so doing, contribute to the social construction of dependency. Practitioners therefore need to be very careful to ensure that the language used, attitudes adopted or steps taken do not infantilise. That is, practice needs to be premised on a model of older people as adults with rights, rather than 'second generation' children.

Dehumanisation is a parallel process in which older people are treated as things, objects rather than subjects, and seen as distinct from 'ordinary' people. According to Thompson (1993, p.86).

> 'There is a strong ideological tendency to dismiss older people, to deny them their humanity. We found a good example of this in an article in a newsletter of a local "Alcohol Forum". The author, a psychiatrist, is discussing safe limits for weekly alcohol consump-

tion when he comments that: "Safety limits are proposed in terms of alcohol units per week (10) but these limits are for males or females, not for the elderly'. Although the good intentions of the author are apparent elsewhere in the article, the common tendency to distinguish between "ordinary people" (that is, males and females) and "the elderly" is clearly in evidence.'

Anti-ageist practice therefore requires a sensitivity to such dehumanising tendencies so that we do not lose sight of the fact that older people are people first and last.

Influencing the practice of others

While a review of our own practice is a necessary condition for developing anti-ageism, it is not a sufficient condition. We also need to consider influencing the practice of others. This is because discrimination and oppression are not isolated incidents of misfortune or bad practice; they are fundamental aspects of the way in which society is organised (Thompson 1993). It is for this reason that we need to develop practice that is anti-discriminatory, rather than simply non-discriminatory. That is, it is not enough to seek to eradicate discrimination from our own practice while condoning it in the practice of others. Practitioners therefore need to develop the skills of:

- recognising examples of ageist practice in the work of colleagues;
- challenging in sensitive and constructive ways;
- promoting an ethos in which anti-ageism is taken seriously and respected;
- being able to deal assertively and constructively with 'counterchallenges'.

Fortunately, although challenging others may be difficult, its impact can be significant. Often, people respond very positively to challenges that are sensitive, constructive and couched in respectful terms, rather than in terms of a personal attack.

Influencing agency policy

The policy level is one that has major implications for practice insofar as it sets the parameters and ethos that underpin practice. There is therefore an important role for practitioners in challenging ageist aspects of policy or procedures, and pressing for the development of an explicitly anti-ageist policy. Admittedly, organisational power structures are likely to be resistant to bottom-up change and, realistically, major changes may not be possible, in the short term at least. However, there is a danger of adopting a defeatist attitude. Acknowledging that change may be difficult, slow and gradual should not be equated with seeing change as a vain hope or impossible dream.

An important strategy is to seek out all possible means of influencing policy. This may be through correspondence (both individually and collectively) with managers, participation in working parties or planning groups, trade union activities and so on. The primary skill is that of being an 'organisational operator' – developing a good understanding of how organisational power structures and channels of influence operate, and recognising opportunities for playing a strategic part in taking them in an anti-ageist direction.

Staff efforts in this regard can, potentially at least, be supplemented by the influence of service users. While working in partnership on a case-by-case basis is an important part of developing anti-ageist practice, the principle can be extended to include the notion of 'participation'. User participation implies being involved at a number of levels, rather than simply planning one's own care. These include planning, monitoring and evaluating services, contributing to policy development, operationalisation and review, and perhaps also contributing to training or even staff recruitment. Where such participation can be encouraged, there is a higher likelihood of ageist policies and practices being identified and challenged.

Developing theory

Traditional theory reflects a medical model of ageing in terms of focusing too narrowly on biological aspects of ageing. However, this is not to say that such theory has no value whatsoever. It is possible for certain aspects of traditional theory to be reworked within an anti-discriminatory framework. We shall give two brief examples to illustrate this point.

Thompson (1991, pp.15–16) presents a case for 'revitalising' traditional crisis theory by amending its basic principles to make them consistent with anti-discriminatory practice:

> '...traditional crisis theory can be criticised for adopting a predominantly white, middle-class male perspective on a range of

issues which relate very closely to structured inequalities and the oppressive social divisions which stack the odds against certain groups in society. An understanding of social disadvantage and discrimination must be incorporated into the theoretical framework if a new crisis theory is to replace the old and thereby make a contribution to anti-discriminatory practice.'

Similarly, Mullender and Ward (1991) argue the case for 'self-directed groupwork' as an approach to groupwork that incorporates anti-oppressive issues and values, and therefore goes beyond the traditional confines of groupwork theory.

These examples demonstrate that some theories at least can and should be developed to incorporate anti-discriminatory practice and, in so doing, present an important challenge to both theorists and practitioners.

Conclusions

This chapter has provided a brief review of some of the challenges posed by the social construction perspective within gerontology. By way of conclusion, some comments will be made about future issues in the experience of old age. First, over the past five years (and partly through the influence) of critical perspectives, greater attention has been given to the extent of diversity within the older population. For example, Blakemore and Boneham's (1993) *Age, Race and Ethnicity*, is an important review of the reality of ageing in a multi-racial society. It documents the various responses to growing old amongst minority groups, and demonstrates the urgent need for more detailed survey and ethnographic research on this topic. Studies in relation to gender and ageing by Arber and Ginn (1995), and by Bernard and Meade (1993), have also provided valuable perspectives on contrasts between men and women, especially in areas such as the experience of poverty, caring and personal relationships. More generally, however, there is a dearth of studies dealing with social class differences in the experience of growing old. Surveys such as the General Household Survey (OPCS 1996) give a hint of some of the material differences in the lives of Britain's older people (as do comparable surveys). However, there is an urgent need for more detailed studies which show the extent to which growing old is shaped by the cumulative advantages and disadvantages of particular class positions. Such investigation is made especially urgent given the growth of inequalities over the past 10 years, especially amongst the older age groups (Rowntree, 1995).

Second, significant changes are also underway in respect of the self-identity of older people. A major component here is the growth of early retirement or early exit from the workforce. At the beginning of the twentieth century, the majority of people continued to work or to look for work until ill-health set in or they reached the point of exhaustion. At the end of the twentieth century, the majority are leaving paid employment well before this point, with a rapid expansion in the number of years currently spent in the period defined as retirement (Laczko and Phillipson 1991). Old age has been dramatically reconstructed in the absence of full employment. This change – in the context of a post-industrial world – is almost certainly irreversible. It is transforming the lives of all older people; it will also affect those who work with them. The opportunities for professional social work with older people will be substantial, albeit that it will be of a very different nature than that which has characterised the past two decades. This chapter has tried to address some of the questions which a future social work will need to address, especially one which challenges the discrimination and oppression faced by many older people.

References

Arber, S. and Ginn, J. (1991) *Gender and Later Life*. London: Sage.

Arber, S. and Ginn, J. (1995) *Connecting Gender and Ageing*. Milton Keynes: Open University Press.

Bengston, V. and Achenbaum, V.W. (1993) *The Changing Contract Across Generations*. New York: Aldeue de Gruyter.

Bernard, M. and Meade, K. (1993) *Women Coming of Age*. London: Edward Arnold.

Biggs, S. (1993) *Understanding Ageing: Images, Attitudes and Professional Practice*. Milton Keynes: Open University Press.

Biggs, S., Phillipson, C. and Kingston, P. (1995) *Elder Abuse in Perspective*. Milton Keynes: Open University Press.

Blakemore, M. and Boneham, M. (1993) *Age, Race and Ethnicity*. Milton Keynes: Open University Press.

Butler, R. (1963) 'The life review: and interpretation of reminiscence in the aged.' *Psychiatry* 26(1), 895–906.

Butler, R. (1987) *Ageism in Encyclopedia of Ageing*. New York: Springer.

Bytheway, B. (1994) *Ageism*. Milton Keynes: Open University Press.

Estes, C. (1979) *The Aging Enterprise*. San Francisco: Josey-Bass.

Estes, C., Gerard, L., Zones, J. and Swan, J. (1984) *Political Economy Health and Ageing*. Boston: Little Brown.

Hockey, J. and James, A. (1993) *Growing Up and Growing Older: Ageing and Dependency in the Life Course*. London: Sage.

Hugman, R. (1994) *Ageing and the Care of Older People in Europe*. London: Macmillan.

James, A. and Prout, A. (1991) *Constructing and Reconstructing Childhood*. London: Falmer Press.

Kingston, P. and Penhale, B. (1995) *Family Violence and the Caring Professions*. London: Macmillan.

Kogan, N. (1979) 'A study on age categorisation.' *Journal of Gerontology 34*, 5, 358–367.

Kuhn, M. (1977) *Maggie Kuhn on Ageing*. Westminster: Philadelphia.

Laczko, F. and Phillipson, C. (1991) *Changing Work and Retirement: Social Policy and the Older Worker*. Milton Keynes: Open University Press.

Langan, M. and Lee, P. (eds) (1989) *Radical Social Work Today*. London: Unwin Hyman.

Midwinter, E. (1992) *Citizenship: From Ageism to Participation*. Research Paper 8, Carnegie Inquiry into the Third Age. London: Carnegie Trust.

Minkler, M. and Estes, C. (1991) *Critical Perspectives on Ageing*. San Francisco: Baywood Press.

Mitchell, G. (1989) 'Empowerment and opportunity.' *Social Work Today*, 16 March.

Mullender, A. and Ward, D. (1991) *Self-Directed Groupwork: Users Taking Action for Empowerment*. London: Whiting and Birch.

Myles, J. (1984a) *The Political Economy of Public Pensions*. Boston: Little, Brown.

Myles, J. (1984b) *Old Age in the Welfare State*. Boston: Little Brown.

Office of Population Censuses and Surveys (1996) *Living in Britain: Results from the 1994 General Household Survey*. London: HMSO.

Phillipson, C. (1982) *Capitalism and the Construction of Old Age*. London: Macmillan Books.

Phillipson, C. (1989) 'Challenging dependency: Towards a new social work with older people.' In M. Langan and P. Lee (eds) *Radical Social Work Today*. London: Unwin Hyman.

Phillipson, C. (1991) 'Inter-generational relations: conflict or consensus in the twenty-first century.' *Policy and Politics 19*, 27–36.

Phillipson, C. (1994) 'Community care and the social construction of citizenship.' *Journal of Social Work Practice 8*, 2, 103–112.

Phillipson, C. and Walker, A. (1986) *Ageing and Social Policy*. Aldershot: Gower.

Rowntree Foundation (1995) *Income and Wealth* (Vols 1 and 2). York: Rowntree Foundation.

Smale, G. and Tuson, G., with Biehal, N. and Marsh, P. (1993) *Empowerment, Assessment, Care Management and the Skilled Worker*. London: HMSO.

Thompson, N. (1991) *Crisis Intervention Revisited*. Birmingham: Pepar.

Thompson, N. (1992) 'Age and citizenship.' *Elders: the Journal of Care and Practice 1*, 1.

Thompson, N. (1993) *Anti-Discriminatory Practice*. London: Macmillan.

Thompson, N. (1995) *Age and Dignity: Working with Older People*. Aldershot: Arena.

Townsend, P. (1981) 'The structured dependency of the elderly: a creation of policy in the twentieth century.' *Ageing and Society 1*, 5–28.

Walker, A. (1980) 'The social creation of poverty and dependency in old age.' *Journal of Social Policy 9*, 49–75.

Walker, A. (1981) 'Towards a political economy of old age.' *Ageing and Society 1*, 73–94.

Walker, A. (1993) 'Poverty and inequality in old age.' In J. Bond, P. Coleman and S. Peace (eds) *Ageing and Society* (pp.280–83). London: Sage.

Ward, D. and Mullender, A. (1993) 'Empowerment and oppression: An indissoluble pairing for contemporary social work.' In J. Walmsley *et al. Health, Welfare and Practice: Reflecting on Roles and Relationships*. London: Sage.

Chapter 2

The Demography of Old Age
Panic Versus Reality

Anthony M. Warnes

This chapter describes the main features of the ageing of the United Kingdom population. The account deliberately mixes conventional demographic reporting with a commentary on society's perceptions of and reactions to the growth of the elderly population. It identifies the most common misunderstandings of the process and their conse-quences. There will be attention to the relationships between age and sickness and disability, partly to assess soberly the implications of further demographic ageing for the medical and social care services and professions. The processes of demographic or societal ageing are those which bring about an increasing average age in a population, an increasing average age of death, and a rising proportion above some arbitrary age, for which the conventional threshold is 60 years.[1] The processes and their implications are not all straightforward and indeed are frequently misunderstood. They produce counter-intuitive facts and trends, and non-specialist discussions are especially prone to several myths and misconceptions. This article attempts to explain how these arise and argues that their effect is to reinforce and disseminate an inappropriately alarmist view of age structure change. In turn the alarmist perception distorts and on occasion demeans the situation and needs of elderly people.

---

1   60 years of age is still useful for international and historical comparisons but its significance as a benchmark of change in people's social roles and activities has to be questioned in every era. During the full employment decades of the 1960s, it did approximate the age among men at which paid work ceased and retirement began. That transition occurs now at more variable and often younger ages. Women's roles, even those who pursue full-time employment, change less abruptly than men's.

Processes and progress of demographic ageing

The rise in life expectancy and the fall in infant mortality

Difficulties begin with the most common explanation of population ageing, namely that 'we are living longer'. While the statement is arithmetically true, it fosters at best simplifications and quite often much misunderstanding. The principal reason for the rise in average life expectancy at birth in Scotland from 50.1 years for males and 53.2 years for females in 1910–1912, to 71.4 for males and 76.9 years for females in 1993 has been enormous decreases in infant mortality (Registrar General Scotland 1994, Table J1.1).[2] By 1993, the annual death rate in Scotland for children aged 0 years was 6.5 per 1000, only one-twentieth (5.1 per cent) of the figure of 126.4 during 1891–1895 (Table 2.1). In comparison, death rates during later working life and the retirement years have fallen less substantially. For example, the annual death rate at ages 65–74 years during 1945–1949 was 46 per 1000, three-quarters of the level in 1901. Improvements at these ages have, however, been accelerating gently, and by 1993 the death rate was down to 35.4, 59 per cent of the 1890s figure. Similar contrasts are shown by the average remaining life expectancies at given ages in England and Wales, for which countries more detailed historical series are collated and published. Life expectancy for men at 65 years of age increased from 10.3 years in the 1890s to 11.7 years in 1950–1952 (+13.6%), and by a further two and a half years to 14.2 years by 1989–1991, a 38 per cent improvement on the 1890s. The equivalent expectancies for females aged 65 years in the 1890s, 1950–1952 and 1989–1991 were 11.3, 14.3 and 17.9 years, a 58 per cent improvement on the 1890s (OPCS 1993, Table 14).

Contemporary accounts of population ageing rarely include appreciation of the fact that the current rate of reduction in infant mortality is higher than ever before and still substantially greater than the improvement in later life mortality. During the 1980s, infant mortality was falling by more than 4 per cent each year, while the death rate at 75–84 years improved by about 1.1 per cent per year. It therefore

---

2   The trajectories of change have been almost identical in other parts of Great Britain and similar in much of north-west Europe: specialist treatments of the variations are available (Chesnais 1986, Warnes 1993). It is worth emphasising that these expectancies are abstractions calculated from the mortality schedules for a particular year (or group of years). They do not represent the mortality conditions experienced by an individual as they age through time.

Table 2.1: Annual age specific death rates
in Great Britain, 1840s – 1990s

Year(s)	SMR[1]	Age group (years) All ages	0–1	55–64	65–74	75–84	85+
I England and Wales							
1841–1845	344	21.4	148	28.7	62.0	137.2	295.3
1891–1895	296	18.7	151	32.5	67.3	140.7	273.9
1951–1955	97	11.7	27	16.6	42.0	105.7	235.7
1971–1975	84	11.8	17	14.9	36.9	87.8	201.0
1981–1985	75	11.7	10	13.4	33.4	78.2	186.3
1991	70[2]	11.2	7	10.9	29.1	71.5	166.4
Compound annual rate of improvement (%)							
1843–1893	0.30	0.27	-0.04	-0.25	-0.16	-0.05	0.15
1893–1953	1.84	0.78	2.83	1.11	0.78	0.48	0.25
1953–1991	0.93[2]	0.11	3.49	1.10	0.96	1.02	0.91
1983–1991		0.54	4.36	2.55	1.71	1.11	1.40
II Scotland							
1855–1860		20.7	119.6	28.1[3]	58.2[3]	155.6[3]	
1891–1895		19.0	126.4	31.2[3]	59.6[3]	139.0[3]	
1945–1949		12.6	53.6	19.5	46.2	110.6	255.8
1965–1969		12.1	22.4	18.1	43.0	99.1	227.0
1985–1989		12.3	8.7	15.6	37.3	82.7	187.2
1993			6.4	13.4	35.4	83.6	194.3
Compound annual rate of improvement (%)							
1857–1893		0.24	-0.16	-0.26	-0.06	0.28	
1893–1947		0.75	1.58	1.65	0.55	-0.13[4]	
1947–1987		0.06	4.44	0.56	0.53	0.72	0.78
1987–1993			4.99	2.50	0.87	-0.18	-0.62

Notes: The death rates are per 1000 people and for both sexes. 1. Standardised Mortality Ratio with base years being 1950–1952. 2. The SMR during 1986–1990 and the rate of improvement during 1953–1988. 3. Data compiled by Flinn (1977, Table 5.5.8, p. 385) for 1861 and 1901. 4. Rate over the period 1901–1931 from Flinn's data

Sources: Office of Population Censuses and Surveys (OPCS) (1989): *Mortality Statistics 1841–1985, Serial Tables,* London: Her Majesty's Stationery Office (HMSO), Table 1; OPCS (1992): *Mortality Statistics 1990: England and Wales, General,* London: HMSO, Table 2; OPCS (1993): *Mortality Statistics 1991: England and Wales, General,* London: HMSO, Table 3; Registrar General for Scotland (RGS) (1922): *Sixty-Sixth Annual Report,* Edinburgh: HMSO, Table 27: RGS (1994): *Annual Report 1993,* General Register Office, Edinburgh, Tables A1.2 and B1.1

remains the case that reductions in infant mortality are a major contributor to the ageing of the population. It follows that to see the process as a 'bad thing' and to argue that it should be restrained is to recommend a slowing of the reduction of premature deaths, especially among children. No explicit statement to this effect has been encountered, but the unintended implication is common.

Increased survival rates in old age

The continuing large contribution of reductions in premature mortality to demographic ageing should be emphasised alongside the spreading recognition that survival in old age increasingly contributes to the average length of life. The contemporary improvements in later-life death rates are, however, continuations of a well-established trend, not, as often described, a remarkably new, unanticipated and mysterious development. Late-age mortality hardly changed during the first three decades of this century, but since the early 1930s steady but gentle acceleration has been evident. The declines in the annual death rate among people aged 85+ years in England and Wales over the four successive twenty year periods from 1911–1915 to 1991 have been 0.85, 7.8, 14.7 and 17.2 per cent (the last figure for the period 1971–1975 to 1991 being over 17.5 years). In Scotland the declines at ages 65–74 years during the successive periods between 1901, 1931, 1955–1959 and 1985–1989 have been 11.7, 12.0 and 19.4 per cent. A similar acceleration has been seen in the United States: on both sides of the Atlantic this acceleration has repeatedly scuppered the conservative mortality assumptions used in population projections. But just because projection methodologists are reluctant to assume anything more favourable than a continuation of the current rate of improvement, i.e. they will not build in accelerating improvement, it does not mean that recent revisions of the anticipated numbers surviving into their eighties, nineties and beyond represent anything unforeseeable or unprecedented, or which should cause alarm about the ensuing necessities of societal adjustment.

Causes of accelerated improvement in survival

The interesting and difficult questions are about the causes of accelerated improvements in later life survival. Many hypotheses and theories are tenable. Those associated with clinical medicine tend first to select explanations to do with the introduction of new treatments and therapies for the most common diseases and causes of death in old age, such as the control of hypertension and the management of heart diseases (Callahan 1987, 1990, Smith 1989). An alternative explanation extends the unresolved controversy about the causes of the epidemiological transition in the causes of (all age) deaths. This transition refers to the reduced lethality of infectious diseases and their replacement as the dominant causes of death by degenerative disorders, notably the heart and circulatory diseases and cancers (Caldwell 1993, McKeown 1988, Olshansky and Ault 1986). Has the change been primarily because of advances in clinical science and practice, or primarily a consequence of direct and indirect improvements in public health (through nutrition, hygiene, preventive medicine, healthy and unhealthy behaviours in-cluding exercise, and housing conditions)? There is no simple or single answer: both sets of changes have made enormous contributions.

It is taken for granted that there was a vast improvement in living conditions in Britain and elsewhere early in this century. The mortality data of Table 1 witness the fact, with infant mortality throughout Great Britain more than halving between 1900 and 1950. People born in the early 1930s and now entering the 60+ years age group benefited from these changes, surely, in many ways, besides their survival. Is it not probable that they experienced fewer childhood privations, better nutrition and better preventive health care than their parents' genera-tion? Do not such life course factors have a substantial influence in current age-specific mortality declines? There have also been many pertinent social changes, as with housing conditions, increased school-ing and changed employment histories, including reduced participa-tion in arduous and hazardous manual work. While longitudinal associations can only rarely be demonstrated from existing social and health data, the proposition that recent improvements in old age sur-vival have much to do with improvements in living conditions throughout people's lives attracts increasing and diversifying attention (Barker *et al.* 1993, Barker 1994, Elmo and Preston 1992, Floud *et al.* 1990). If these propositions are true, then even if advances in the treatment and management of diseases of later life ceased, the survival of people in and through old age would continue to improve.

The influence of fertility rates on ageing populations

A second misinterpretation of the reasons for population ageing com-monly arises from the explanation that 'we are all living longer'. It is the misleading extension that the increased duration of life longevity is the principal reason why the older age groups form a growing share of the total population. As all demographic text books make clear, the main determinant of a population's age structure is the level of fertility. Put simply, a high birth rate produces a large share in childhood and a low share in old age, and a low birth rate, as seen in Europe today, produces a low share in childhood and raised shares in working and retirement ages. It follows that the main reason for the enormous change in British and European age structures over the past 120 years has been the collapse of fertility to near, or as in several nations, below, replacement levels.

Our societies are greatly confused about what is 'good' and what is 'bad' about the current demographic regime. During the 1960s the unprecedentedly high rate of growth of the world's population stimulated widespread analysis and concern, particularly in connection with the consumption of non-renewable resources and damage to the world's ecology. The alarmists succeeded in persuading public opinion in the western world (although not all demographers or development economists) that reductions in population growth were desirable: some neo-Malthusians argued that they were essential for our long-term survival. Previously, as in France during the nineteenth century, natalism or the promotion of population growth was the more common nationalist view. Reactions to the subsequent declines in fertility in Europe, the resulting population decreases in Germany and Scandinavia, and the prospect of the same in France have, to date, been muted. Some environmentalists continue to argue that the reductions are desirable, but politicians will be increasingly reminded of a relation between population size and the total gross domestic product. For as long as a nationalistic competition for population size is suppressed and it remains politically incorrect to advocate a higher birth rate and population growth, commentators will complain about the symptom of infertility, an ageing population.

Other misinterpretations are that the ageing of the British population is (a) something rather new and (b) set to continue indefinitely and with ever increasing momentum. No empirical data or projections support this simplicity, which forms when an historical perspective mixes with extrapolation of short-term trends. In fact, the age structure has been changing throughout this century in response to the decreases in fertility after the 1870s. The most rapid rates of change were during the middle decades of the century (Table 2.2). Taking the number aged 60+ years, the annual rate of increase was greatest during the 1920s (2.2%). For the 70+ years population, the fastest increases were during 1931–1951, and for the 80+ years, during 1931–1961. The pace of change has slowed considerably over the last two decades. A detail meriting wider dissemination is that during the 1980s the population in Great Britain aged 60–69 years decreased by 43,000 (Table 2.2). That fall, associated with fewer births during the 1910s compared to the first decade of the century, will manifest itself during the 1990s among people in their seventies, and during the first decade of the next century among those in their eighties. It is true that there will be a resurgence of elderly population growth from around 2005 for two decades, as the high birth cohorts of the period 1945–1965 reach 60 years of age. But few accounts trace the connection between the record of births and the fluctuating number achieving old age. Instead, the tendency is to present demographic ageing as a boundless prospect.

**Table 2.2: The changing number of elderly
people by age: Great Britain, 1901–1991**

	Population (thousands)				Share of total (percentage)			Annual growth (%)		
	60+	70+	80+	All ages	60+	70+	80+	60+	70+	80+
1901	2876	1066	218	38,237	7.5	2.8	0.6	–	–	–
1911	3434	1298	251	42,082	8.2	3.1	0.6	1.8	2.0	1.4
1931	5314	1962	376	46,038	11.5	4.3	0.8	2.2	2.1	2.0
1951	7890	3399	730	50,225	15.7	6.8	1.5	2.0	2.8	3.4
1961	8973	3954	1017	52,709	17.0	7.5	1.9	1.3	1.5	3.4
1971	10,512	4599	1263	55,515	18.9	8.3	2.3	1.6	1.5	2.2
1981	11,020	5438	1485	55,089	20.0	9.9	2.7	0.5	1.7	1.6
1991	11,713	6174	1824	56,388	20.8	10.9	3.2	0.6	1.3	2.1

Source: Falconer and Rose (1991), Table 1.2; Central Statistical Office (1994): Annual Abstract of Statistics 1994. London: HMSO, Table 2.5
© Crown copyright.

Inculcating a long view of the ageing of the British population will encourage more critical reactions to assertions of unbounded and continuous increases (or even worse accelerating growth) in the elderly population. Such presentations often use 2030 as the final date of their projections.[3] During the 2020s, the 1960s high birth cohorts will enter their seventh decade of life. Consequently, the decade will see an exceptionally large increase (projected to be 14.9 per cent) of the 60–69 years population. Rarely presented, however, is that during the following decade the low 1970s birth cohort will reach their seventh decade and so the population aged 60–69 years is projected to fall, not by a small margin but by 1.57 million or 19.4 per cent. During the 2030s and subsequent decades, there may as a result be difficult issues of retrenchment in some services for older people. Thirty-five years is a long way ahead, but whether witting or unconscious there is a touch of deception in spotlighting the 2020s without mentioning the prospects beyond. The target date 2030 maximises the prospective rate of increase and is therefore most useful to those keen to demonstrate a 'tidal wave'. These include an unlikely coalition between political parties and ideologues who wish to reduce social security provision and taxation, and health and social service professionals who wish to demonstrate an exceptional need for increased resources. Projections to only 2010 or beyond 2030 are far less impressive.

Late-age mortality trends and population projections

The absolute and relative size of the future elderly population cannot be known precisely. Although many projection figures are published and they are widely reproduced, actual population figures always diverge from them. Projections are as good as the assumptions about fertility, mortality and sometimes migration built into them, and therefore as good as our understanding and models of recent trends. That understanding has been improving fast but remains rudimentary (Olshansky 1988). The perennial difficulty of population forecasters has been to anticipate fertility – birth rates in this century have been notably fickle. In comparison, demographers have for long seen mortality as subject to relatively steady decline, but the trends have recently altered. To the growing awareness of the gentle acceleration of late-age mortality decline has recently been added evidence of increases in male death rates in early adulthood (Daykin 1994):

---

3   During the week before completing this paper I attended a meeting at which five slides showed elderly population projections. All used the target date of 2020 or 2031.

Table 2.3: Population projections, United Kingdom 1991–2041

Age	1991		2001		2011		2021		2041	
(years)	m	fm	m	fm	m	fm	m	fm	m	fm
Thousands										
0–15	5675	5377	6033	5726	5419	5403	5508	5250	5194	4953
16–44	12,677	12,430	12,483	12,129	12,381	11,660	11,698	11,203	11,052	10,601
45–59	4736	4776	5528	5614	6105	6203	6284	6273	5725	5584
60–64	1393	1501	1403	1457	1843	1928	1861	1956	1628	1649
65–69	1291	1503	1231	1331	1466	1566	1546	1674	1584	1653
70–74	983	1299	1048	1262	1124	1262	1494	1690	1637	1815
75–79	727	1136	811	1141	847	1048	1062	1280	1404	1692
80–84	419	829	475	843	554	855	666	907	921	1263
85–89	180	466	230	548	291	600	359	595	522	839
90+	50	201	92	332	128	426	179	494	409	863
60+	5044	6934	5291	6914	6252	7685	7167	8598	8105	9775
75+	1377	2632	1609	2864	1819	2930	2266	3277	3256	4658
Total	**28,132**	**29,517**	**29,335**	**30,383**	**30,158**	**30,952**	**30,657**	**31,324**	**30,075**	**30,912**

Table 2.3: Population projections, United Kingdom 1991–2041 (continued)

Age	1991		2001		2011		2021		2041	
(years)	m	fm	m	fm	m	fm	m	fm	m	fm
Percentage of total population										
0–15	20.2	18.2	20.6	18.8	18.0	17.5	18.0	16.8	17.3	16.0
16–44	45.1	42.1	42.6	39.9	41.1	37.7	38.2	35.8	36.7	34.3
45–59	16.8	16.2	18.8	18.5	20.2	20.0	20.5	20.0	19.0	18.1
60–69	9.5	10.2	9.0	9.2	11.0	11.3	11.1	11.6	10.7	10.7
70–79	6.1	8.2	6.3	7.9	6.5	7.5	8.3	9.5	10.1	11.3
80–89	2.1	4.4	2.4	4.6	2.8	4.7	3.3	4.8	4.8	6.8
90+	0.2	0.7	0.3	1.1	0.4	1.4	0.6	1.6	1.4	2.8
60+	17.9	23.5	18.0	22.8	20.7	24.8	23.4	27.4	26.9	31.6
75+	4.9	8.9	5.5	9.4	6.0	9.5	7.4	10.5	10.8	15.1

Source: OPCS (1993), Appendix I.

'For men between the ages of 24 and 46 mortality rates are tending to rise at present, largely due to deaths arising from HIV infection, but also from an increasing number of suicides and accidental deaths...Past and current trends suggest that those now over about age 47 will continue to show, in each cohort, lower mortality rates than in the preceding cohort...this has been their experience to date and at present their mortality rates are diminishing by between one and four per cent a year. This trend has been strong for nearly two decades... It has therefore been decided to assume, in general, rather greater improvement than in the previous projections for all those born in 1945 or earlier.' (OPCS 1993, p.8)

Revising assumptions

The current difficulty facing forecasters is therefore novel, to anticipate the duration, pace and age distribution of the accelerated mortality declines among the older age groups, and at what age there is a 'flip' to the less favourable trends found among middle and young adults. The latest 1991-based projections to 2031 (with extrapolations to 2061) use substantially revised assumptions – the previous significant revision was in 1985. Of most influence upon the projected size and age structure of the UK population, 'the assumed long-term family size for the United Kingdom as a whole has been reduced from 2.00 to 1.90 children per woman'.

A selection of the new official projections is given in Table 2.3. These suggest that the United Kingdom population aged 60+ years will exceed 12 million during the 1990s and in the early decades of the next century enter a period of faster growth, to 15.8 million by 2021. During the 2030s the growth phase will end and it is expected that during 2041–2061 the 60+ years population will fall by 6 per cent to 17.1 million. As a result of the low fertility assumption, during this period the total population is likely to be falling and the elderly population will continue to grow as a share of the total. In 2031 they are likely to form 29.1 per cent of the total, and by 2061 to be 29.8 per cent. An increasing average age is projected among the elderly population, and the numbers aged over 75 years and over 85 years will grow more quickly than the entire elderly population.

The technical standards of official population projections are very high and the care and responsibility displayed are exemplary. The problem of misinterpretation is among secondary users, who see the projections as firm predictions, do not study the assumptions, and select the figures which most support their argument. My own critique of the assumptions built into the latest British projections highlights two things: the sensitivity of the age group share to the very low fertility assumption, and the continuing refusal to incorporate a gently accelerating rate of mortality improvement in later life, even among those now aged 47+ years. It cannot be argued that different assumptions are more correct – it is just a personal view that these critical assumptions are very frail.

Age, health and health care demands

In the health and welfare services the lazy labelling of the collectivity of patients or clients as 'the elderly' is well known. Most enunciators are intellectually aware that the majority of older people (including their own relatives and friends) are healthy and independent, but this apparently harmless term circulates easily among young staff. The problem is that the stereotype encourages the false and damaging notion that sickness and problems are indelibly associated with old age, and therefore the extension that our growing ageing population is problematic and a burden. In a single year only about one-fifth of the population aged 65+ years consult a general practitioner or receive a visit from a district nurse, and nearly three-quarters have 'no chronic or long-standing disease' or 'ones which have no effect on daily life' (Falconer and Rose 1991).[4] In the Oxford Region, person-based annual rates of admission to hospitals during 1979–1986 were approximately eight people per 1000 aged 60–64 years, rising to around 25 per 1000 at ages 80–84 years (Carnegie UK Trust 1993). There is, of course, a high prevalence of sickness and disability in old age, and many disorders have geometrically rising prevalence to high levels among nonagenarians and centenarians, but most older people are not disabled and it is false to categorise them as such.

---

4   Falconer and Rose use various tables (not all specified) from the *Health and Lifestyle Survey 1984–85, OPCS Morbidity Statistics from General Practice* and successive *General Household Surveys*. For updated data see Cox, Huppert and Whichelow (1993), OPCS (1993), OPCS (1995) and OPCS (Annual). Other useful compendia on the health and social welfare dependency of elderly people are Grundy (1992), Carnegie UK Trust (1993) and Central Health Monitoring Unit (1992).

The effects of lifestyle changes

The existence of progressively rising functions of incidence and prevalence is one foundation for further simplistic reasoning, that as the absolute and relative size of the population who survive into their eighties and nineties increases, then we can project future health and social welfare demands by applying today's prevalence and service provision rates to the raised totals. There are two flaws in this procedure. First, the incidence and prevalence of at least some conditions is particular to each birth cohort, as is most widely accepted for the relation between lifetime tobacco consumption and the risk of various cardiovascular diseases. Actuaries are presently forecasting declines in the age–specific male death rate from heart disease, as a result of the decline in cigarette smoking. Some disorders may be related to early and adult nutrition and to lifestyle (e.g. osteoporosis), some may be related to exposure to pollutants and toxins (e.g. various respiratory disorders), and some may be reduced in disabling effect by improved diagnoses and treatments (e.g. various neoplasms and hormone replacement therapy for osteoporosis).

The second flaw is that for a large volume of health and social service activity, although not the most glamorous or high cost examples, provision is less a function of 'absolute need' than a consequence of policy and funding decisions. These are influenced by actual and perceived expectations and demands from the general public, the advocacy of service professionals and their representative bodies, and the priorities and ideological principles of the government of the day. Just as the recent reductions in the number of older patients in mental hospitals is not a sign of a reduced prevalence of mental illness, nor is the growth in the number of older people living in residential and nursing homes a function of rising disability or dependency. Over the last decade there have been increasing efforts to collect robust data on the prevalence of sickness and disability in the population. Our knowledge is improving slowly, but the data now available are readily misused. The validity, or actual meaning, of some temporal series still needs careful evaluation. Several items asked in the General Household Survey are subject to the difficulties of all self-ratings of health and functioning, and others reflect policy changes and service expansion rather than objective health status.

Self-rated health and changing expectations

Self-ratings of health are conditional on not only the age of the respondent but also the 'health norms and expectations' of the time. In 1972, 13 per cent of boys aged 0–4 years were seen by GPs, but by 1989 the share had nearly doubled to 24 per cent – it is worth noting that over the same period the consultation rate of 75+ years old males (19%) changed not at all (OPCS Monitor SS90/3, 30 October 1990, Table 16). The General Household Survey has found a steadily increasing fraction of the population reporting a limiting long-standing illness, and the younger the adult age, the faster the climb. From 1972 to 1989, the positive reports increased from 14 to 24 per cent of those aged 16–44 years, while among females aged 75 years it increased from 65 to 70 per cent. No one could believe that the trend in young adults measured 'objective health status', and therefore the small increase among the population in advanced old age should not be interpreted as such or as a firm basis for projecting rising disability in the future. Important research in both the United States and in the United Kingdom is seeking to establish trends in age-specific disability and ill-health. The methodological and information difficulties are immense, and for some time to come the results should be treated with great caution. Those who confidently assert that there is evidence of rising age-specific morbidity are either naive or have a professional or political interest in doing so.

Sources of alarm

Several simplicities and misconceptions concerning population ageing have been mentioned in this chapter. The most conspicuous have been that:

- The main reason for the increases in life expectancy in Britain during this century have not been because adults are living substantially longer but because fewer babies die in the first year of life.

- The main reason for the massive increase in the share of the population that is elderly is not because adults live longer but because the birth rate has fallen to a very low level.

- Population ageing did not begin in the last few years but has been proceeding since the beginning of this century and the fastest rates of change in the age structure were during 1921–1951.

- United Kingdom population projections do not anticipate ever higher numbers of older people but instead approximate stability during the 2030s and the onset of significant declines after 2046.

- The main causes of recent increases in health care expenditure are expanded services to all age groups, the introduction of new treatments including medications, and the labour-intensive nature of the service. The contribution of age structure changes (and therefore of the rising number of older people) makes only a minor contribution to these costs.

Conclusions

However unlikely it may seem today, a recovery of the birth rate is possible and it does not have to be huge to reverse the age structure trend. There have been two previous surprises in the fertility history of the twentieth century in Britain: the high birth rates from the early 1950s to the late 1960s (after four decades of low fertility apart from the anticipated brief periods of post-war recovery), and the precipitate fall of the birth rate in the early 1970s. Responding to the first change, theorists of fertility encompassed notions of children as consumption goods, for which the demand increased with affluence as for motor cars and holidays. When the adverse economic conditions of the early 1970s resulted in sharp declines in fertility in the majority of the developed nations, those ideas became less popular and more emphasis was given to the costs of raising children. What will be the next surprise?

Alarm about the implications of demographic ageing is more intensive and widespread in the United States than in Britain or the rest of Europe. This is partly because the American elderly population is growing faster (throughout this century their birth rates have been higher than Europe's and there has been from decade to decade substantial immigration). Another reason is that the Federal commitments to Medicare, Medicaid and the US Social Security Budget have produced a rapidly rising bill which conflicts directly with the goals of the resurgent Republican Party. Third, the organisation of the United States health care system, and its greater concern, when compared to the National Health Service, to meet 'market demands' rather than to raise treatment standards for all, has heightened a perception of potentially escalating costs associated with new, high technology treatment. The problems surface as 'alarm about ageing' when arguably they are mainly matters of social and health policy and administration. Unfortunately, however, our media commentators are greatly influenced by American analyses and opinion: we can all be infected.

The implications of demographic ageing on British health and social services are more often exaggerated or misrepresented than carefully appraised. Policy changes, such as the re-structuring of residential care and community health services, and the progressive specialisation of hospitals as centres of acute services with little place for continuing, palliative or nursing care, are a greater source of managerial strain and resource scarcity than the changing number of older people. And the most challenging long-term trend is the rising health and care expectations of the population – babies, children, adolescents and adults of all ages. The older population has in fact been relatively restrained in its growing demands for treatment in comparison to other age groups. To see the pressures on our services or their rapid rates of change as largely a consequence of population ageing is often facile and sometimes dissembling. More rigorous analyses and prognoses should be sought.

References

Barker, D.J.P. (1994) *Mothers, Babies and Disease in Later Life.* London: British Medical Journal Publishing.

Barker, D.J.P., Gluckman, P.D., Godfrey, K.M., Harding, J.E., Owens, J.A. and Robinson, J.S. (1993) 'Fetal nutrition and cardiovascular disease in adult life.' *Lancet 341*, 938–41.

Caldwell, J.C. (1993) 'Health transition: the cultural, social and behavioural determinants of health in the third world.' *Social Science and Medicine 36*, 2, 125–35.

Callahan, D. (1987) *Setting Limits: Medical Goals in an Aging Society.* New York: Simon and Schuster.

Callahan, D. (1990) *What Kind of Life: The Limits of Medical Progress.* New York: Simon and Schuster.

Carnegie UK Trust (1993) *Health, Abilities and Well-Being in the Third Age.* Dunfermline: Carnegie UK Trust.

Central Health Monitoring Unit (1992) *The Health of Elderly People: An Epidemiological Overview, Volume 1* and *Companion Papers*. London: Her Majesty's Stationery Office.

Chesnais, J-C. (1986) *La Transition Démographique*. Paris: Presses Universitaires de France.

Daykin, C.D. (1994) 'The recent trend of mortality in the United Kingdom.' *Journal of the Institute of Actuaries 121*, 3, 589.

Elmo, I.T. and Preston, S.H. (1992) 'Effects of early life conditions on adult mortality: a review.' *Population Index 58*, 2.

Falconer, P. and Rose, R. (1991) *Older Britons: A Survey.* Studies in Public Policy 194, Centre for the Study of Public Policy, University of Strathclyde, Glasgow.

Flinn, M. (ed) (1977) *Scottish Population History from the Seventeenth Century to the 1930s.* Cambridge: Cambridge University Press.

Floud, R., Wachter, K.W. and Gregory, A. (1990) *Height, Health and History: Nutritional Status in the United Kingdom, 1750–1980.* Cambridge: Cambridge University Press.

Grundy, E. (1992) 'The epidemiology of aging.' In J.C. Brocklehust, R.C. Tallis and K. Traske (eds) *Textbook of Geriatric Medicine,* 3rd edition. Edinburgh: Churchill Livingstone.

McKeown, T. (1988) *The Origins of Human Disease.* Oxford: Blackwell.

Office of Population Censuses and Surveys (OPCS) (1993) *National Population Projections: 1991-Based.* Series PP2, no.18. London: HMSO.

Olshansky, S.J. (1988) 'On forecasting mortality.' *Milbank Quarterly 66*, 482–530.

Olshansky, S.J. and Ault, A.B. (1986) 'The fourth stage of the epidemiological transition: the age of delayed degenerative diseases.' *Milbank Memorial Fund Quarterly 64*, 3, 355–91.

Registrar General for Scotland (1994) *Annual Report 1993.* Edinburgh: General Register Office.

Smith, G.T. (1989) *Measuring Health: A Practical Approach.* Chichester, Sussex: Wiley.

Warnes, A.M. (1993) 'Demographic ageing: trends and policy responses.' In D. Noin and R. Woods (eds) *The Changing Population of Europe.* Oxford: Blackwell, 82–99.

Chapter 3

The Financial Circumstances of Older People

Christina R. Victor

Introduction

When considering the financial circumstances and living standards of older people, there are two distinct and contrasting images which may be identified. The first casts older people as being almost inevitably poor and points to a causal relationship between low income and later life. A more recent image is diametrically opposed to this and emphasises the affluence of later life and of older people. It is this perspective which has generated the image of the *woopies* (well off older people) and the *joolies* (jet setting oldies with loads of loot). This chapter attempts to look behind these stereotypes and present the real financial situation of the older age groups and the subgroups into which they may be divided. We examine the financial circumstances of older people in Britain in several different ways. In the first section, we examine some of the methodological issues concerned with looking at the financial situation of older people (and indeed other age groups). Section two reviews the sources of income available to older people, while in section three we describe their financial circumstances and the different components into which these may be broken down. Section four looks at the different sources from which older peoples's incomes are derived and these are then compared with the incomes of people of working age. Finally, we consider whether older people are becoming better (or worse) off.

Definitions and concepts

Within the space of a single chapter it is not possible, nor is it appropriate, to provide a detailed examination of the methodological prob-

lems involved in the description and analysis of the financial circumstances of a particular segment of our population. However, in order
to make sense of the data presented and the debates which now
surround issues like the financial position of older people, it is first
necessary to highlight some of the underlying issues and define the key
terms and concepts.

The first issue to be confronted in reviewing the financial situation
of older people is 'what is an older person?' How is this particular
subgroup of the general population to be defined? Most of the data
concerning the financial situation of older people are derived from
Government statistics and surveys. A key term within these sources is
that of 'pensioner'. However, this could mean those who are receiving
state retirement pensions, those who are retired or those who have
reached the age of 60/65. It may also mean 'pensioner units' which
could embrace single people over retirement age, a couple in which the
man is over 65, a couple where either one (or both) of the partners
receive the state pension. Given the variety of different meanings which
an apparently identical term can have, it is little wonder that there are
such profound disagreements as to the real financial situation of older
people.

Another issue to be confronted is the way that income is defined in
the various studies and data sources. Income may be calculated gross
or net of tax and national insurance; it may also be defined as gross or
net of housing costs and it may (or may not) be adjusted for the different
size of households.

A final issue to be addressed is the way that information about
income is presented. A commonly used way of describing income is as
a mean (or average) figure. This measure is not necessarily the most
appropriate way of describing the distribution of income within a
population as it is artificially inflated by the presence of large incomes
(even though they may be received by only a few people). The median
income is the amount which divides the distribution in half; 50 per cent
will have incomes above this level and 50 per cent will have incomes
below this level. An example of how the use of these two different
measures may give a different picture of the financial situation of older
people is provided by Hancock and Weir (1994). They report that the
weekly average income (net of tax and adjusted for household size) of
pensioners (those aged 60/65+) in 1989 was £107 while the median was
£83, a difference of £24 a week.

Interpreting official statistics and other sources of data describing the financial situation of older people (or, indeed, other segments of the population such as lone parents) is therefore fraught with problems. In the substantive sections of this chapter the evidence presented about the financial circumstances of older people is mostly derived from the analysis of two main surveys undertaken by the Office of Population Censuses and Surveys (OPCS) on behalf of the Government. These are the Family Expenditure Survey (FES) and the General Household Survey (GHS).

Income sources in later life

Before considering the substantive topics of this chapter, it is first necessary to describe the main sources of financial support for the older age groups. Older people who remain active in the formal labour market will be in receipt of earnings from employment. Those not gainfully employed are dependent upon two main sources for their income: pensions and savings. Pensions may be received from two main sources; the state national insurance scheme, and pensions from previous employers (occupational pensions). The fairly recent establishment of personal pension schemes means that those who have taken out this form of pension provision have not yet reached retirement age. Consequently, this recent development does not feature in this analysis. Each of the two main forms of pension provision are briefly described below, as are the other sources of income in later life, as an understanding of the main sources of income available to older people is an essential pre-requisite to understanding their financial circumstances.

State national insurance pension provision

The state national insurance retirement pension is known colloquially as 'the old age pension' and the current scheme has been in operation since 1948. It is payable at a flat rate to all those who have finally retired from the labour market provided that they have the appropriate national insurance contributions, approximately 44 years for a man and 39 years for a woman. Almost half of the social security budget is spent upon older people. The largest slice, £8.6 billion in 1987/8, is used to fund the state retirement pension (Hancock and Weir 1994).

The State Earnings Related Pension (SERPS) was devised in 1978 to provide an additional pension for those who did not have the opportunity to contribute to a private or occupational pension. As a result of the review of social security payments in 1984, the value of the payments made under this scheme will be downgraded as it was perceived as being 'too generous'. The graduated pensions benefit based upon contributions made between 1961 and 1975 is virtually negligible. In the subsequent analysis, data are usually presented for all sources of income deriving from the state, as few sources distinguish between the different origins of this income.

Means-tested benefits for older people

For those older people with an income below a defined level, additional pensions and benefits are payable. Up to April 1988, this was known as supplementary pension and was the arm of the means-tested Supplementary Benefit system catering for older people. Since April 1988 this has been replaced by Income Support. This is received by a considerable number of older people. Age Concern (1994) report that, in 1992, 1,414,000 single people aged 60 and over, and 229,000 couples were receiving Income Support. A further £1.1 billion finances supplementary pensions.

In addition, older people may also be in receipt of Housing Benefit or Community Charge Benefit. In 1992, 1,961,000 people over 60 were receiving Housing Benefit and 3,057,000 were receiving Community Charge Benefit. Clearly some people were receiving more than one benefit. Age Concern (1994) report that in 1991, 2,800,000 people aged 60 and over, and 1,069,000 couples were receiving more than one income-related benefit.

Other state benefits

Older people may be in receipt of some disability-related benefits such as Invalidity Benefit, Severe Disablement Allowance, Disability Living Allowance and Attendance Allowance. These benefits are not intended to provide recipients with higher standards of living but rather to compensate them for the 'extra' costs of their disability. According to Age Concern (1994) there were 720,000 people aged 65 and over receiving Attendance Allowance in 1992.

Occupational pensions

As noted earlier, few of those who have taken out personal pension plans have yet reached retirement age. The OPCS retirement survey which was carried out in 1988/89 revealed that only 6 per cent of those aged 55–69 had such a plan and only 1 per cent were actually in receipt of the pension derived from this source (Bone *et al.* 1992). However, as future cohorts of people retire from the labour market personal pensions will become an important component of income in later life for at least some groups of pensioners.

In Great Britain in 1992, 62 per cent of male full-time employees were in an occupational pension scheme and 27 per cent had a personal pension; for women full-time employees the percentages were 54 per cent and 21 per cent respectively. However, for women part-time workers only 19 per cent had an occupational pension and 12 per cent had a personal pension (OPCS 1994). There has been remarkably little change in recent decades in the percentage of the workforce in occupational pension schemes. In 1979, 64 per cent of male full-time workers had an occupational pension as did 47 per cent of full-time women workers compared with 62 per cent and 54 per cent respectively in 1992 (OPCS 1994). For both full-time male and female employees the percentage of people in either occupational pensions or with a personal pension increases with the amount of income that they earn. Fifty per cent of men and 40 per cent of women earning under £100 a week in 1992 had an occupational pension (and 20% and 18% respectively a personal pension) compared with 80 per cent and 82 per cent respectively of those earning over £300 a week (for personal pensions the coverage was 24% and 23% for men and women) (OPCS 1994).

Generally, occupational pensions are based upon the final earnings of the individual as it is assumed that this will be their best earnings level. This assumption is not always true for some groups of employees. Furthermore, as these pensions are related to levels of earnings it is obvious that they reproduce employment income inequalities into the post-retirement phase of life.

Age Concern (1994) estimate that approximately 56 per cent of pensioner families (either single people or couples in which at least one partner is over retirement age) receive an occupational pension. We shall explore the importance of occupational pensions to the financial well-being of older people in a later section.

Earnings

Few people of retirement age are active in the labour market. Given the trend towards early retirement which has become more prevalent in the past decade, it seems unlikely that income from employment will be a major source of income for older people in the future.

Other sources of income in later life

Older people may have savings or investments which will yield income during retirement. This may be termed unearned or investment income. In 1989, Age Concern (1994) report that, overall, 75 per cent of pensioners have some investment income. This varies from 87 per cent of pensioner couples to 69 per cent of single pensioners. Some older people may also receive financial support from relatives but it is difficult to quantify this source of income.

The financial circumstances of older people

In this section we shall consider the financial situation of pensioners in Great Britain. Table 3.1 describes the mean and median incomes of single pensioners and pensioner couples. Taking the median as our indicator of weekly income, single pensioners have an average annual income of just under £4000 (£3910.40) and £7207.20 a year for couples. Single pensioners have approximately half the income of pensioner couples. However, for both groups the arithmetic average (or mean) gives a more flattering view of pensioner incomes than does the median income. For single pensioners the difference is £19.60 a week and for couples it is £42.60 a week.

Table 3.1: Net weekly income of pensioners – 1990/92 before housing costs

	Mean	Median
Single pensioners	£94.80	£75.20
Couples	£181.20	£138.60

Source: Age Concern England 1994, Table 1.1

Table 3.2 presents more detailed information about the financial circumstances. Because of the range of incomes it is useful to group individuals into categories of income. Usually five groups or quintiles

Table 3.2: Average gross weekly income 1989 – by quintiles

	bottom 20%	2nd 20%	3rd 20%	4th 20%	top 20%	total	ratio of bottom and top (%)
Single	£50.70	£62.60	£71.00	£86.40	£199.20	£93.90	392
Couples	£88.20	£106.50	£130.50	£176.60	£396.00	£179.40	449

Notes: In 1989 the basic pension for a single person was £43.60 and £69.80 for couples

$$\text{Ratio} = \frac{\text{bottom quintile}}{\text{top quintile}} \times 100$$

Source: Age Concern England 1994, Table 1.2

are used. The bottom quintile represents the bottom 20 per cent of the income distribution, the second quintile is the next poorest 20 per cent, whereas the top quintile represents the 20 per cent of people with the highest incomes. Table 3.2 presents information about the mean income of the five quintiles for pensioners in 1989. In interpreting this table it is helpful to remember that in April 1989 the basic pension was £43.60 for a single person and £69.80 for a couple, and average annual adult earnings were £12,464 a year. The average annual income for pensioners in the bottom 20 per cent of pensioner incomes was £2,636.40 for single people and £4,586.40 for couples, as compared with £10,358.40 and £20,592.00 respectively for those in the top 20 per cent. Those at the top of the income distribution have incomes approximately four times larger than those in the bottom 20 per cent.

Another indirect indicator of the financial situation of older people is the amount (if any) of income tax paid by this group. Of the approximately nine million people aged 60/65 in Britain about one third (3 million) were liable for tax. Estimates from Age Concern (1994) suggest that 120,000 people (about 1.3%) paid tax at 40 per cent rate which suggests a taxable income in excess of £23,700 a year, and 1,490,000 were basic rate taxpayers.

Distribution of income between older people

As with other subgroups within our population, income is not equally distributed between all members of the older population. Rather, the elderly population is characterised by profound differences in both financial and material circumstances of the different groups which combine to form 'the elderly population'.

Throughout this chapter we have distinguished between single pensioners and pensioner couples. Table 3.2 shows that single pensioners have incomes which are approximately half that of pensioner couples. The more favourable financial circumstances of pensioner couples reflects their younger age distribution and the fact that within a couple there is more chance of receiving income from additional non-state sources.

As Table 3.3 illustrates, median weekly income decreases with age. For both men and women aged 80+ their weekly income is 77 per cent of that for those aged 65–69. Hancock and Weir (1994) also draw attention to the more favourable financial circumstances of the newly retired, as compared with those who have been out of the formal labour market for longer. The more favoured financial circumstances of the 'younger' elderly has been reported elsewhere (see Falkingham and Victor 1991). However, this observation is not a reflection of ageing *per se* but reflects the differential access of young and old pensioners to non-state sources of income.

Table 3.3: Median weekly income of pensioners by age and sex – 1989

	Male	Female	Male/ Female ratio
60–64	–	£104	–
65–69	£97	£87	111
70–74	£88	£77	114
75–79	£74	£68	108
80 +	£75	£67	111

Source: Hancock and Weir, Table 2

$$\text{Male/Female ratio} \quad \frac{\text{male income}}{\text{female income}} \times 100$$

The situation of women

Furthermore, at all ages, women have an income which is approximately 10 per cent lower than that of men of their own age. Arber and Ginn (1991) argue that the low incomes received by women in later life represents a continuation of the pattern seen at earlier phases of the life-cycle and is a pattern which has also been reported in North America. They consider that women's lower income in later life is a result of their lower incomes while in employment, their lower rates of employment reinforced by pension schemes which assume women's dependence upon men and which are based upon the assumption of an uninterrupted employment history.

In North America, elders from minority communities are at much greater risk of experiencing low income and poverty in later life than is the white population (Arber and Ginn 1991). It seems likely that a similar pattern applies to older people from minority communities in Britain, although there is little empirical evidence yet to support this supposition. There are also social class differences in the financial circumstances in Great Britain. However, data describing the extent of these differences are not routinely published. Victor (1987) reports that the median weekly income in 1980 of people aged 65+ from social class 1 and 2 (the professional occupation groups) was almost treble (2.89 times higher) that of their counterparts in classes 4 and 5 (the semi- and unskilled manual groups).

Who is most at risk of low income in later life?

Without digressing into a discussion of the definition of poverty in late twentieth century Britain, we can identify those subgroups within the older age groups who are most at risk of experiencing poverty and low income in later life. From the analysis presented above we may conclude that women, those living alone, those aged 80 and over and those from unskilled or semi-skilled jobs are most at risk of experiencing low income in later life. Similarly, Hancock and Weir (1994) note that those living alone, females and those aged over 80 are over-represented amongst the bottom 20 per cent of the income distribution.

Sources of income in later life

In an earlier section we described the various sources on which older people may depend for their income in later life. Furthermore, we have already alluded to the importance for older people of non-state sources of income in later life. In this section we shall explore how important different sources of income are to older people. Most older people are in receipt of income from state sources (this includes both the retirement pension and other benefits). However, as Table 3.4 shows, only half of all older people receive an occupational pension and two-thirds have income from savings or investments. The amounts of money recipients obtain from the different sources is indicated in Table 3.5. However, we may calculate this in two different ways: for all older people or for only those older people who actually receive income from each source. Scrutiny of Table 3.5 reveals that, overall, the largest sums received by older people derive from the State. However, we see that there are marked differences in the mean and median amounts received from non-state sources if we compare calculations for all pensioners and all pensioners receiving income from these sources.

Table 3.4: Access to different sources
of income for single pensioners and couples – 1989 (%)

| | *% with income from sources* | |
	Single pensioner	*Pensioner couples*
State benefits	99	99
Private pensions	44	72
Occupational pensions	42	70
Savings	57	77
Earnings	6	12
Other	3	3

Source: Hancock and Weir (1994), Table 11

Table 3.5: Components of pensioner incomes 1989 – receipt
of gross income from different sources – 1989

| | | *Amount received weekly* | | | |
| | *%* | *All pensioners* | | *Recipients only* | |
Income type	*receiving*	*Mean*	*Median*	*Mean*	*Median*
State benefits	97	£71	£62	£73	£62
All private pensions	54	£37	£5	£69	£35
Occupational pensions	52	£33	£2	£65	£35
Savings	65	£24	£2	£37	£10
Earnings	13	£24	£0	£188	£109
Other	3	£2	£0	£64	£27

Source: Hancock and Weir (1994), Tables 7 and 8
Notes: Pensioner unit is either a single person or a couple in which either or both
partners are of state pension age

If we concentrate upon two non-state sources of income, occupational pensions and savings/investment income, Table 3.5 shows that 50 per cent of those who have savings derive less than £10 a week from this source. Similarly, less than half of those with an occupational pension get less than £35 a week from this source. Consequently, many of those with investment or non-state pensions receive relatively small sums from these sources.

What is the importance of state and non-state sources of income in later life? Johnson and Falkingham (1992) estimate that, overall, approximately 60 per cent of pensioner income is derived from the state, 20 per cent from occupational pensions, 14 per cent from savings/investments and the rest from employment. However, the importance of state and non-state sources of income varies across the income distribution. Johnson and Falkingham (1992) report that 90 per cent of the income of older people in the bottom 20 per cent of the income distribution is derived from the state, compared with 25 per cent for the top 20 per cent. Indeed, even for pensioners with incomes in the 60–80 per cent of the income distribution, the 4th quartile, nearly two-thirds (65%) of income is derived from state sources. For the bottom 20 per cent of pensioners 3.5 per cent of income is derived from occupational pensions and 5.7 per cent from savings/investments. For the top 20 per cent of older people these percentages were 30.8 per cent from both sources.

These data indicate that for the vast majority of older people their main source of income is derived from state sources. For only a minority – those at the very top end of the income distribution – do non-state sources contribute any significant amount. Detailed research reveals that single pensioners, women and very elderly people are most reliant upon the State for the bulk of their income (Arber and Ginn 1991).

The non take-up of state benefits

Despite the fact that considerable numbers of older people receive means-tested additional benefits, it is clear that many do not claim all the benefits to which they are entitled. It is estimated that between one-third and one-fifth of pensioners eligible for Income Support do not claim this benefit (Age Concern 1994). We may speculate that the underclaiming of other benefits by older people is probably of the same order of magnitude. Atkinson (1991) estimated that one-fifth of all pensioners entitled to means-tested benefits were not claiming them.

Why do older people not claim all the benefits to which they are entitled?

The reasons for the non take-up of benefits are many and complex. One factor is clearly the complexity of the claiming process. The Income Support claim form for older people is 24 pages long, with additional pages if the applicant wishes to claim Housing Benefit. Clearly, the length and complexity of such a form might be a disincentive to claiming benefits. Other factors implicated in the failure of older people to claim benefits include perceived stigma associated with 'means-tested benefits', not wishing to claim while they are 'managing' financially and problems with the actual process of claiming.

How does the financial situation of older people compare with the rest of the population?

There is a substantial body of research comparing the income of the retired population in Britain with those below retirement age (see Hancock and Weir 1994). Optimistic statements from government sources suggest that the real incomes of the retired are increasing and that this group is improving its economic position with regard to the rest of society (DHSS 1995). An important focus of attention in the debate about social policy as related to older people has been the relationship of the income of the retired as compared with the non-retired. This change in emphasis away from concerns about the widespread prevalence of poverty in old age has been viewed as part of a larger concern that Britain has become 'too equal'. In this section we are concerned with the position of older people relative to the rest of the population. In the next section we shall consider whether older people have been getting better (or worse) off in recent years.

Older people and poverty

The poverty statistics are cited in support of the view that older people are becoming better off in relation to the rest of society. In 1970, pensioners constituted 64 per cent of those claiming Supplementary Benefit compared with 39 per cent in 1989 (Falkingham and Victor 1991). However, this change has been brought about almost entirely by the increase in the long-term unemployed rather than by an increase in the living standards of older people in the lowest income groups. Rather, it reflects the creation of an even poorer group, the long-term unemployed, who have very low incomes.

Data about the distribution of low income in Great Britain are published by the Department of Social Security (1993). They provide data about the composition of the groups which have incomes below the average (mean) for the population as a whole. In 1990/91 17 per cent of single pensioners and 20 per cent of pensioner couples had incomes above the national average (adjusted for family size). The percentage of pensioners with incomes below average was 34 per cent among single people and 33 per cent for couples. This indicates that the vast majority of pensioners have average or below average incomes. Similarly, when the characteristics of those in the bottom 20 per cent of the national income distribution (adjusted for family size) are examined we find that 39 per cent are retired households, as are 47 per cent of the next 20 per cent (CSO 1995). From this we may conclude that older people constitute one of the poorer segments of society.

Little has changed from the early research of Townsend (1979) when he described the number and characteristics of older people living at the Supplementary Benefit (now Income Support) rates or their margins (i.e. within 140% of the relevant rate). He reported that 20 per cent of those aged 65 and over were living in poverty and another 44 per cent were living on the margins of poverty. From the analysis of the differential access of older people to non-state sources of income in later life presented earlier, it comes as little surprise that Townsend showed that it is the very old (i.e. those aged over 80), women, those living alone and the disabled who are most at risk of experiencing poverty in later life. Low social class, interrupted employment patterns and lifelong 'low' social status are also important risk factors when considering the prevalence of poverty in later life.

Affluence in later life
However, in 1990/91, 7 per cent of people in the top 20 per cent of the national income distribution are pensioner households. So clearly there are some older people represented within the highest income groups within Great Britain. The study of income distribution within the older age group has concentrated upon describing the prevalence of low income and poverty. There has been much less investigation of wealth and high income and its prevalence among older people. The absence of studies of wealth amongst older people is not a feature unique to later life. Rather, it reflects a bias within social research towards considering the position of the underprivileged rather than privileged

members of the population. However, Falkingham and Victor (1991) report that it is men, those under 75 and those from professional occupations who are most likely to be well off older persons (woopies!).

Are older people becoming better or worse off?

One of the fiercest debates in recent years has been concerning the relative income position of older people. It is certainly true that the incomes of older people have increased over recent decades. Hancock and Weir (1994) report that average pensioner incomes increased by 27 per cent between 1979 and 1989 (from £84 a week to £107 a week). However, during the same period mean non-pensioner incomes increased by 30 per cent. If we examine median incomes, then pensioner incomes increased by 15 per cent and non-pensioner incomes by 24 per cent. Over this period the disadvantaged position of women, those aged over 75 and those living alone has been accentuated. While there has been little improvement in the position of older people relative to those in employment, older people have improved their position relative to other recipients of state benefits, such as the long-term unemployed.

Discussion

In this brief review of the financial position of older people several points arise. There is considerable diversity in the incomes of older people. This is not a new finding but it is worth reiterating. Within the elderly population certain subgroups, women, those aged 75 and over, those living alone and those in non-manual occupations are at most risk of experiencing low income in later life. While during the past decades pensioner incomes have increased, they have not increased as much as those in employment, and neither have these increases been equally distributed across all pensioners. It is men and younger pensioners who have benefited most from increases in pensioner incomes.

Inequality in income amongst older people seems to be on the increase. Given that the value of the state retirement pension is decreasing it seems likely that such inequality will increase in the future. Although we are all being exhorted to take out occupational pensions, current evidence suggests that occupational pensions are not a guarantee of affluence in later life. Many occupational pensions, or indeed investments, do not yield sufficient income in later life to compensate for the declining role of state pensions. Given the complexity of the circumstances of people as they enter into old age it is difficult to be prescriptive about developing policy towards income maintenance in later life. The reality remains that for most older people, later life is a time of low income and financial deprivation. However, there is an important role here for social work/services departments as well as voluntary organisations in mitigating some of the poverty experienced by older people. By informing them about the range of state benefits to which they may be entitled and by offering assistance with the claiming process, the numbers of eligible non-claimants may be reduced. We already know that there is a considerable amount of underclaiming of benefits by older people, and appropriately targeted welfare rights advice could make a positive contribution towards improving their financial circumstances, thereby enhancing their quality of life.

References

Age Concern (1994) *The Pensions Debate: A Report on Income and Pensions in Retirement*. Age Concern England.

Arber, S., Ginn, J. (1991) *Gender and Later Life*. London: Sage.

Atkinson, A. (1991) 'The development of state pensions in the United Kingdom.' Welfare State Discussion Paper No.58, LSE.

Bone, M., Gregory, J., Gill, B. and Lader, D. (1992) *Retirement and Retirement Plans*. OPCS. London: HMSO.

CSO (1995) *Social Trends*. London: HMSO.

DHSS (1995) *Reform of Social Security: Background Papers*. London: HMSO.

DSS (1993) *Households below Average Income: A Statistical Analysis 1979–1990/91*. London: HMSO.

Falkingham, J. and Victor, C. (1991) 'The myth of the woopie.' *Ageing and Society 11*, 4, 471–493.

Hancock, R. and Weir, P. (1994) *More Ways than Means: a guide to pensioners' incomes in Great Britain during the 1980s*. London: Age Concern Institute of Gerontology.

Johnson, P. and Falkingham, J. (1992) *Ageing and Economic Welfare*. London: Sage.

OPCS (1994) *General Household Survey 1992*. London: HMSO.

Townsend, P. (1979) *Poverty in the United Kingdom*. Penguin.

Victor, C.R. (1987) *Old Age in Modern Society* (1st edition). Beckenham, Kent: Croom Helm.

Chapter 4

Social Services for Older People in Europe

Alan Walker

Introduction

Social services are in transition throughout the European Union. The recent combination of various pressures – socio-demographic, fiscal, ideological, grassroots – has begun to produce reforms, or proposals for reform, in all EU countries. Reforms include the creation of more mixed economies of welfare, the separation of provider and funding roles, care-packaging, case management and the tailoring of services to users (Friedmann, Gilbert and Sherer 1987, Evers 1991), though the extent and pace of change in social services is by no means uniform across member states. In the interests of promoting the development of more effective and better quality systems of care for older people, it is important to understand the scope of the reforms and to build on the most progressive features of them, even though in some cases the ideological engine driving them may be antithetical to this goal (Walker 1989).

The aims of this chapter are two-fold. The first is to examine the degree of convergence between member states of the EU in their policies and practices towards the care of older people; and, second, to outline the challenges facing social services over the next decade or so. This analysis inevitably raises the issue of the EU's competence in this field and, specifically, how far the development of its social policies will generate convergence among the fifteen national social services systems, and I will return to this matter by way of a conclusion. As a starting point, here is a very brief summary of the main organisational features of social services in EU countries focussing on domiciliary care.

Organisation of home care services in the EU

There is considerable institutional variation between member states, including a range of different funding arrangements, so caution is necessary in making international comparisons. Also, until recently, there was very little comparative information on personal social service provision in the EU. That deficiency has been rectified to a considerable extent by a series of cross-national research projects on the care of older people in EU countries, most of which were sponsored by the European Commission. These include the joint Leuven-Amsterdam comparative study of services in the twelve countries of the European Community (Nijkamp *et al.* 1991); the Age Care Research Europe project covering nine countries (Jamieson and Illsley 1990, Jamieson 1991); the European Centre's study of service innovations in The Netherlands, Sweden and England and Wales (Kraan *et al.* 1991); the Hoger Institute's research (Pacolet, Versieck and Bouten 1994); and the early stages of the comparative research of the EU's own Observatory on Ageing and Older People (Walker, Guillemard and Alber 1991, Walker, Alber and Guillemard 1993).

The most common approach to the organisation of domiciliary care in the EU is for these social services to be clearly differentiated from medical services and under the control of local authorities. Home care services in the EU are at varying stages of development and three broad groups of countries may be distinguished: those with fully developed services in terms of scope and coverage, those with partially developed domiciliary service infrastructure; and those where services are underdeveloped. (As will be seen later in this chapter, even in those countries with fully developed home care services by no means all domiciliary care needs are being met, and regional disparities in provision are common).

Looking first at those countries with fully developed home care services, in *Belgium*, services have been organised on a regional basis under the control of local authorities and non-profit voluntary associations since 1982 (while health care is centralised). The main domiciliary services are home helps and cleaning services, district nursing, meals on wheels and day centres. *Denmark* has the most fully developed system of domiciliary care services in the EU. The main services provided are home helps, district nursing, meals on wheels and social work. All services are co-ordinated and administered by local authorities and financed from taxation. The home help service covers household management tasks, such as cleaning, and personal care including hairdressing, assistance with eating and dressing. In most municipalities the home help service is available on a 24-hour basis and is combined with district nursing in the same organisational unit. The development of home care services in *France* may be split into two periods, pre- and post-1983. Since 1983 these services have been increasingly regionalised under the control of local branches of national government. Home helps are financed from social assistance and pension insurance. In *Luxembourg* home help and home nursing have been long established as the main domiciliary services and they are run almost wholly by private and non-profit organisations. The Family Ministry co-ordinates and partly pays for services going to low-income families. The major providers of home nursing services are religious orders, the Red Cross and two municipalities. Meals on wheels have been introduced recently but day centres are scarce and emergency telephones are found only in the capital. Until recently the bulk of social services expenditure in the *Netherlands* went to residential care but increasing amounts of home care are being provided to substitute for residential care. Domiciliary care is supplied by local non-profit associations and financed (up to a limit) by an exceptional medical expenses scheme with private cost-sharing. The *United Kingdom* would also be classified as a country with a fully developed social services system, as would the new EU members, Austria, Finland and Sweden.

Turning to those countries with partially developed systems, in *Germany* (former FDR) home helps are financed by means-tested social assistance and provided by the voluntary sector with public subsidies. *Italy* is still in transition from institutional to community care. Domiciliary services are organised by local health units, financed from regional funds. Provision is patchy and inadequate in many places, especially in the south. Community care policy towards older people in *Spain* developed in three stages: prior to 1972 there were no social policies for older people, between 1973 and 1979 policy concentrated on residential homes, and from 1979 local personal social services have been created, including home helps and day centres. Domiciliary services are organised by local authorities and voluntary associations and financed by municipalities for low-income users.

Finally, there are two countries with underdeveloped domiciliary services. The last decade in *Greece* has seen the development of community services around the KAPI system (i.e. decentralised community centres and informal care) supplemented by district nurses, home helps, meals on wheels and physiotherapy, but provision is minimal. *Portugal* has placed increased emphasis on day centres for older people (there are 530 such centres) but domiciliary services are in very short supply. Where these services exist they are financed partly from social security and partly from private charges.

Care of older people in the EU: current trends

Despite considerable institutional variations between EU countries, particularly on the north/south axis, it is possible to identify five major common trends and themes in the current development of policies towards the care of older people.

The State preference for community care

Not only are at least some community care services for older people available in all EU countries, but all governments are expressing a preference for this form of care as opposed to residential or hospital care. In some cases this preference has been a long-term one. The various reasons for this policy are outlined below but, for the moment, it is important to recognise that because the motivations behind this policy vary between countries, the nature, the pace and scale of the changes underway, or being contemplated, differ significantly between countries. Thus, among the long-established institutional welfare states of the Northern part of the EU, we may contrast the market-orientated thrust of the British government's community care policy – privatisation, the creation of quasi-markets in social care and the withdrawal of local government from the direct provision of services – with the careful attempts to reform the state agencies themselves in Denmark.

These sorts of variations derive from fundamental differences in ideologies between the governments in power in member states rather than from any intrinsic features of their social services. But, in addition, as shown above there is considerable variation between EU countries in the organisation and level of development of social services. For example, in administrative terms, the home help/home care services in Greece and Portugal are combined with district nursing and, in Belgium and the Netherlands, there are additional cleaning services. There are also some variations in the classification of home care tasks as being either primarily nursing or domestic in nature. The dominant model of care in the EU appears to be the conventional home help role consisting of, on the one hand, practical care and tending, primarily in household management and domestic tasks and assistance with other activities of daily living; and on the other, emotional support – being concerned, befriending, acting as adviser or confidant (Warren 1990). Moreover, in the majority of EU countries home care provision is either public or predominantly public; at the present time there are very few for-profit agencies. The Swedish model of home care appears to be more flexible, covering housekeeping and personal care as well as some straightforward medical tasks.

The clear preference on the part of EU governments for the community-based care of older people is also shared by EU citizens. In the recent Eurobarometer survey in all 12 member states a large majority of the general public (four out of five) thought that older people should be helped to remain in their own homes (Walker 1993a, p.29). The only countries wherein more than one-fifth of the general public preferred residential accommodation to community care were Denmark and Portugal.

Shortages of community care personnel

While there is a clear convergence in political rhetoric concerning community care, there are wide variations in provision between EU countries. The range stretches from more than one home help for every five households headed by a person aged 65 and over in Denmark, to 1 in 10 in France, 3 in 100 in Ireland, 1 in 100 in Spain, to 1 in 200 in Portugal. Denmark and the Netherlands and, to a lesser extent, the UK seem to be the countries with the most extensive infrastructure of services among the Northern EU countries. For example, Denmark has 27,000 people employed in home care services (35 per 1000 people aged 65 and over). Whereas in Germany there are only 22,000 full-time equivalents or 2.4 per 1000 people aged 65 and over. The proportion of older people in receipt of services is smaller than these figures suggest because the home care jam is not spread uniformly across the older population in any country. Swedish home care provision is closer to the Danish levels than those of other EU countries (Kraan *et al.* 1991).

Thus, even in some of the major EU countries, the levels of domiciliary care services are not sufficient to keep pace with the rising need created by socio-demographic change. In other words, there is a 'care gap' between the need for care among older people and the supply of both informal and formal carers (Walker 1985, Qureshi and Walker 1989). It has both demand side and supply side components (Nijkamp *et al.* 1991, p.270). This care gap is a feature of the majority of EU countries, all of whom except Denmark and Luxembourg report excess demand, and there are growing concerns about the lack of specialist services for older people with dementia. Surprisingly, there are also signs of a care gap in Sweden (Kraan *et al.* 1991, p.190).

The continuing failure to provide sufficient community care services obviously means that some frail older people and their family carers are put under intolerable strains which, in turn, threaten the viability of their caring relationships. It means too that the social services cannot realise their full potential in the prevention of dependency but, instead, are forced to act in a reactive or casualty mode – a point I return to later.

Territorial inequalities

There are considerable territorial variations in the coverage of social care services *within* EU countries. In some cases these regional disparities appear to be of the same magnitude as some of those between the north and south of the EU. For example, in Italy there is not a full home care service in all of the country's 21 regions, and in France and the UK there are wide differences in provision between different areas. Geographical isolation is a factor in such territorial inequalities but it is not the major one. For example, in the UK there is wide variation in home help numbers between local authorities, depending on their political complexion: within London some boroughs provide three times as many home helps per 1000 older people as others. Even in Denmark and Sweden there are regional variations in home care provision, partly resulting from their highly decentralised systems.

Fragmentation of community care

In most EU countries there is fragmentation of community care policies: public, private and voluntary agencies, and, as a consequence, lack of co-ordination between domiciliary care and other services. Most important of all there is the separation between health and social services. Whereas health services are financed from social insurance or general taxation, social services are usually administered and financed either by local government or by various voluntary organisations or a combination of both.

So the necessity of integrating the services is impeded by the organisational separation of responsibilities for funding and management. Most countries report problems of co-ordination between health and social services and these appear to be particularly acute in Belgium, Germany, the Netherlands and the UK. The main exception is Ireland, where health and social services are managed by the same department at local level.

The problem of lack of co-ordination in the face of ever-increasing demand has led to adaptations being made to services in some countries. For example, in Italy some social workers are acting as social network organisers. In Belgium co-operation initiatives between GPs, home help services and district nursing have been introduced. In France there are regional coordinators, in Luxembourg the integration of all services in regional centres for older people is intended to enhance co-operation and in the Netherlands there are neighbourhood health centres.

Service innovations

What is, perhaps, most striking about the comparative EU research is that despite, or rather because of, shortages of funding, the social services are in a state of purposive development. Examples include:

- service buses – Ireland, the Netherlands;
- the spread of alarm systems – in Belgium, France, Luxembourg, the Netherlands, Spain, Sweden and the UK;
- hospital at home/terminal care schemes – the Netherlands;
- hospital discharge schemes – the UK;
- the increasing recognition of and support for informal carers including self-help groups in Belgium and Sweden; carers' support groups in Belgium, the Netherlands, Sweden and the UK; family placements/boarding out in Germany, Greece, Ireland and Italy and the UK; respite care in Belgium, the Netherlands, Sweden and the UK; sitting services in Belgium and the UK;
- short-term or supplementary home care – the Netherlands;

- new community resources in support of home care, such as day centres in Belgium, France, Ireland, Luxembourg, the Netherlands, Portugal, Sweden and the KAPI in Greece;

- housing improvements – Denmark, the Netherlands and the UK;

- new forms of service integration and co-ordination in Belgium, France, Ireland, the Netherlands and the UK;

- new training regimes to improve the quality of home care services in Denmark and Luxembourg.

While there is plenty of evidence of considerable innovatory zeal throughout the Community it is important to guard against the danger of over-emphasising the impact of service innovations. Despite the existence of high profile innovations throughout the EU (and beyond) the dominant model of social care remains that of the traditional home help. In other words, the experience of the majority of older people who are fortunate enough to be receiving social services amounts to one or two hours per week of home help. Change is taking place even within the social services, for example, the enhanced home care/community support worker role in the UK and Denmark, but the 'spotlight effect' of innovations should not mislead us into imagining that they are universal.

So, it is necessary to be cautious in concluding that evidence of innovation means that the majority of older people in the EU are receiving an adequate home care service – this is very far from being the case, even in the long-established welfare state societies.

Pressures for change in social services

This brief review of current trends in the provision of domiciliary care reveals both convergence and divergence: there is a remarkable degree of similarity between member states in the sort of traditional services available to older people but considerable disparities in the level of such services. With the exception of Denmark, the Netherlands and the UK (together with Austria, Finland and Sweden) the northern EU states are characterised by minimal home care provision (with a wide variation in the definition of 'minimal'); while the southern states and Ireland suffer from underdevelopment in all social services. Nonetheless, it is possible to discern similar trends and service developments within the Community as a whole. This is not surprising perhaps because some of the pressures for change facing member states are common ones. There are three main sources of pressure:

Socio-demographic pressures

The European Union is ageing rapidly. At present there are 48 million people aged 65 and over in the EC, 20 million of whom are aged 75 or over. By the year 2000 they will represent more than one-fifth of the population and by 2020 they will comprise more than one-quarter. All EU countries face similar demographic patterns: lower fertility rates coupled with higher life expectancy – though they have different starting points. There is considerable convergence between member states in the proportion of their populations aged 65 and over.

The facts of the demographic revolution are well known so I will not labour the point, but it is important to guard against the tendency to regard population ageing automatically as a problem (Henwood and Wicks 1984, Phillipson and Walker 1986). Ageing populations are a sign of success – mainly on the part of national health services and especially public health measures – in overcoming many of the causes of premature death that cut short people's lives in the last century. Moreover, even among the very elderly it is still only a minority that require care (one-third of those aged 80 and over in Germany and the UK).

But population ageing does present a challenge to the social services, partly because of the association between disability (including dementia) and advanced old age, and partly because this change is coupled with other socio-demographic changes.

Most importantly there is the fertility trend towards smaller family size. This means that by far the main source of care for older people in need – their own families – are having more and more to face the prospect of caring for older relatives for longer and with fewer potential family members to help. Moreover, since women are the main source of care within the family, smaller families mean that more and more women are being forced to shoulder both the labour and the responsibility for caring, on their own (Qureshi and Walker 1989). This development is of profound importance for both families and the providers of home care and other services.

It means that family members are entering new inter-generational caring relationships – new in terms of both their intensity and duration – with both sides having to bear the strains these relationships can generate (Walker 1993b). The inevitable result is that these caring relationshps will break down with increasing frequency, due to carer fatigue. Alternatively, given this prognosis fewer and fewer women will be prepared to enter such long-term caring relationships. Either way, the result is increased demand for service provision (often residential). There are very few examples of care systems having fully adjusted to the implications of the demographic revolution that we are experiencing currently.

The trend towards increased female participation in the labour market (often in roles, such as home care, that mirror their domestic one) puts additional burdens on the female-dominated informal care sector. Although there is no widespread evidence at present that women are giving up family care for the labour market, the case of Denmark gives some indication of the potential conflict between full time paid employment and unpaid domestic labour. In 1960 one quarter of women aged 25–34 were employed. By 1986 this had risen to 89 per cent (Dooghe 1991). At the same time Denmark is the one EU country to report relatively low 'family' participation in care (Walker, Guillemard and Alber 1991). The example of Denmark gives some flavour of the distaste of Scandinavian women for the full-time housewife role (Waerness 1990) and, therefore, the enlargement of the EU is likely to emphasise further the social distance between north and south. The growth in divorce and family break-ups is also important because there is evidence that divorced children give less help to older relatives than those in stable marriages. As well as providing less direct personal care they are less likely to have social contact with their older relatives (Cicirelli 1983).

There is one further point of importance in this socio-demographic matrix. In all EU countries an increasing proportion of older people are living alone. This is partly a function of demographic change and geographical mobility, but it also appears to reflect a desire for separate dwelling places on the part of both older and younger people. The variation in the EU is from a low of 17.5 per cent of people aged 65 and over living alone in Ireland to a high of 49.3 per cent in Denmark. Again, it is necessary to be cautious about this trend. There has been a great deal of speculation about the break-up of the family which is simply not borne out by the evidence. What the research shows is that, although they may live in separate households, older people and their adult children are still in close contact – they prefer 'intimacy at a distance' (Qureshi and Walker 1989, Walker, Guillemard and Alber 1991).

So caution is necessary, but the widespread trend towards living alone has service implications: older people living alone are likely to be poorer than couples and in some countries, such as the UK, social services have traditionally been targetted on (or rationed to) those living alone.

Political/economic pressures

In all EU countries economic concern about the cost implications of population ageing – in terms of pensions, health and social services – is coupled with political worries about the fiscal implications of increased welfare spending. In some countries this has led to a high level of pessimism about the so-called 'burden' of societal ageing (Walker 1990). In general, economic concerns about the cost implications of population ageing are universal – however, the more extreme forms of pessimism are associated primarily with those governments that, for ideological reasons, have adopted an anti-welfare state posture.

The service implications of these political/economic pressures are, as far as the mild form found in most EU countries is concerned, a cost-effectiveness imperative that, for example, establishes the principle that older people should stay in their own homes for as long as possible and promotes a search for cheaper forms of care. In the extreme pessimistic form of these pressures there is a desire to place even greater responsibilities on family members and to encourage the growth of the private and voluntary sectors in substitution for the public sector. Scandinavian countries are not immune to these pressures but, so far at least, they have taken the relatively mild forms of action with regard to social care (Waerness 1990, Kraan *et al.* 1991).

Within the EU the specific service implications of these political/economic pressures include: strict financial limits on care (Belgium, France, Greece, Ireland, Italy, the Netherlands and the UK); a shift or a planned shift from residential to community care (all countries but most radical in the Netherlands because the proportion of older people in residential care has been, on average, twice as much as other countries); deinstitutionalisation (Ireland, Germany, the Netherlands and the UK); increased expectation of financial contributions (Belgium, Germany, Italy and the UK); decentralisation (Germany, Ireland, Italy, the Netherlands and the UK); encouragement of family and informal service networks (Germany, Ireland, the Netherlands); failure to improve training and pay for home care staff, which reinforces staff shortages (most countries); local experimentation with cheaper forms of care (most countries); encouragement of the private sector (Italy, Luxembourg, the Netherlands, Portugal and the UK).

Thus, although they are not the only factors underlying the new agenda in services for older people, political and economic pressures are key inspirations behind innovation and experimentation. In other words, if necessity is the mother of invention, then the primary necessity in EU countries is shortage of funds.

Grassroots pressures

In the Northern EU states with long-established social services systems a certain disillusionment with these services has set in recently, particularly with regard to monolithic public services. These services, including traditional home care services, have been subjected to four sorts of criticism.

USERS

First, more and more users of the social services have been complaining about their bureaucratic organisation, complexity and lack of responsiveness to felt needs. In fact, there is a long series of research studies pointing to the divergence between the perceptions of need held by users and professional providers in the social services (Mayer and Timms 1970, Sainsbury 1980, Fisher 1989). Some groups of users – such as people with disabilities – have formed self-advocacy movements to press their case for greater influence over their own lives and the services they use. At the present time groups of older people are not at the forefront of pressure for change in the social services, but the recent emergence of grey political parties and the strengthening of EU wide organisations of older people suggests that this may change in the future.

WOMEN

Second, there is the distinct feminist critique of the gendered nature of care which has developed, since the late 1970s, into a devastating indictment of both informal and formal care. Feminists have been primarily responsible for demonstrating that community care is, in fact, mainly care by female kin and also that care consists of two dimensions: labour and love (Land 1978, Finch and Groves 1980, Walker 1981). This has led to a demand for alternative approaches that do not exploit women (Dalley 1983, Finch 1984, Waerness 1986). Of course, this criticism is of direct relevance to traditional home care services because they are modelled largely on the female domestic or housewife role and are staffed mainly by women. Furthermore, many innovations in social care rely on the unpaid or low paid services of women and, therefore, they may be subjected to the same feminist critique as traditional social services.

CARERS
Third, out of this feminist critique has come a specific case mounted by those people responsible for providing informal care. During the 1980s, in Britain and the Netherlands, carers began to form self-help and pressure groups to support themselves and represent their views. Together with researchers they have shown, for example in the UK, that community care policies have paid very little attention to the needs of carers and the state has done very little to support the activities of the 6 million carers (Oliver 1983, Wright 1986). The EU is likely to see the emergence of more politically active informal carers as more women enter the labour market and more men take on caring roles. Their pursuit of their own and their relatives' interests will inevitably put further pressure on services.

Informal (unpaid) carers are part of the 'taken-for-granted' context within which services are provided (Twigg, Atkin and Perring 1990). For example, the provision of home care is based to some extent on assumptions about the availability of informal carers and their domestic duties towards the person in need of care. Thus the scope of home care is determined frequently by the activities performed, or assumed to be performed, by a caring relative. If home care services are targetted on those living alone and without relatives living nearby, then those carers often under the greatest strain (those living with a frail older person) will not receive the support they need (Levin, Sinclair and Gorbach 1985).

BLACK AND ETHNIC MINORITIES
Fourth, users and carers from ethnic minority groups have begun to criticise the social services in general and the home care services in particular for failing to recognise their specific needs and the extent to which their cultural background and their experience of racism should be reflected in service provision (Atkin 1991).

These four criticisms are contributing to a disillusionment with social services, including traditional home care services, and, in combination with the demographic, political and economic factors, have created significant pressures for change in the organisation and delivery of services. They have set a new agenda for the care of older people and other groups (Evers 1991). Some changes are already underway, for example:

- standard, off-the-peg, services are being replaced by more flexible, 'tailor-made' and co-ordinated care services;
- the role of the informal sector is becoming more explicit and attempts are being made to integrate better the formal and informal, rather than seeing them as substitutes for each other;
- in some cases the service user as a passive recipient is being replaced by the idea of an active co-producer of welfare;
- symbolically the term 'client' is being replaced by 'user'.

These are, of course, desirable changes because they mean that services can begin to reflect better the needs of users and informal carers.

But the progress of change across the EU is patchy and still the majority of older people who are fortunate enough to receive services will not be aware of any new agenda. This raises questions about the prospects for the emergence of an EU wide convergence in policies on the care of older people.

Towards a European policy on the care of older people?

The goal of extending domiciliary care for older people is explicit throughout the EU. But, at the same time, we have seen that home care services are in short supply in virtually all EU countries and only in Denmark and Sweden is there a widespread 24-hour service. Thus, there is a continuing care gap and many home care services are still stuck in a traditional mould. At the same time most older people in need of care have very little choice, if any at all, about the service they receive (both in terms of the type of service and its intensity). The signs of overburdening can be seen in the incidence of physical and mental ill-health among informal carers (and in sickness rates and absenteeism among paid home carers).

How should EU countries respond to the pressures I have outlined? What is the role of the Commission itself in encouraging convergence towards best practice in the social care of older people? It must be recognised that the primary motivations behind change in the social services are political and economic rather than grassroots. Thus, one of the most important and difficult challenges facing policy makers and service providers is how to create a more equal and effective partnership with the citizens they serve. Of course the answer to this challenge has profound implications for the meaning of citizenship to older people and their carers and, in particular, how much power and autonomy they are able to exercise in making decisions about their own needs and the sorts of services they require. In other words, how far can the political and economic pressures for change be steered in the positive direction of empowering service users and carers, or are these elements of the new agenda entirely incompatible?

It is possible to envisage forms of care provision in which older users and their carers are involved at every level of service planning and delivery (Croft and Beresford 1990, Walker 1992). However, there is substantial institutional inertia standing in the way of this user involvement and empowerment. In addition there are even more formidable political and ideological barriers confronting the introduction of users' rights and empowerment. If the primary motives behind the promotion of community care are political and economic, then the added encumbrance of more costly user-representation and advocacy machinery is not likely to be favoured by national governments. Also, user empowerment fits uneasily with the two extremes of current welfare state governance in Europe. On the one hand there is the paternalistic tradition of the Nordic Welfare states and, on the other, there is neo-liberalism, found in its extreme form in Britain but in watered-down versions elsewhere, which deprecates welfare rights and is opposed to the further development of public services. However, it must be said that rights are (or have been) more commonly associated with Scandinavian welfare states than with other forms of welfare state.

What hope is there that the EU itself will act as a major source of pressure towards convergence in user-orientated social services? The main difficulty is that the Commission has no legislative competence in this field. Indeed, until very recently it had taken hardly any action at all with regard to older people. In discussions concerning the Internal Market of 1992 older people have been largely invisible and the Social Charter or Chapter is primarily concerned with those in employment.

Moreover, the agreement on EU social policy at Maastricht shifted the emphasis in social security from harmonisation to convergence. Thus the principle of subsidiarity is likely to rule out the granting of any powers to the Commission with regard to the care of older people. But this does not mean that the Commission has no role to play, far from it. The Maastricht Treaty gave the Commission some competence in the field of public health and the second programme on ageing (due to be ratified in June 1995) includes specific mention of good practice with regard to the care of disabled older people. Thus the Commission has a vital task to perform in publicising examples of good practice – in service provision, training and so on – and encouraging the standardisation of vocational qualifications, in order to facilitate the convergence of social services towards a model that enhances the status of older people in the EU by ensuring that they are treated with respect and dignity. The Commission also has an important contribution to make in research and monitoring and the encouragement of knowledge transfer. The sharing of knowledge North/South and South/North is particularly important in order to ensure convergence within the EU, in so far as convergence is possible in the context of very different cultures.

Conclusion

Considerable convergence has already taken place in the social services of member states towards an increased emphasis on community care. This will undoubtedly lead to improvements in care for some older people but provision in most countries is likely to remain minimal. There is little realistic hope of a massive and widespread growth in home care, for example, to harmonise with Danish, Dutch or Swedish levels of provision. There is even less chance of the voluntary sponsorship of user empowerment by national governments, or in the medium term, by the EU Commission. The best that we can hope for in the short-term is to build on good practice in service innovations, while in the long-term the growing political confidence of older people's organisations in Europe may well bear fruit. Their campaign for equal EU citizenship, perhaps in combination with domiciliary care providers and their organisations, could produce a radical new agenda in the care of older people: one based on users' rights rather than providers' discretion.

References

Atkin, K. (1991) 'Health, illness, disability and black minorities: a speculative critique of present day discourse.' *Disability, Handicap and Society 6*, 1, 37–47.

Cicirelli, V. (1983) 'A comparison of helping behaviour to elderly parents of adult children with intact and disrupted marriages.' *The Gerontologist 23*, 619–625.

Croft, S. and Beresford, P. (1990) *From Paternalism to Participation*. London: Open Services Project.

Dalley, G. (1983) 'Ideologies of care: a feminist contribution to the debate.' *Critical Social Policy 8*, 72–81.

Dooghe, G. (1991) *The Ageing of the Population in Europe*. Brussels: CBGS.

Evers, A. (1991) 'Introduction.' In R. Kraan, J. Baldock, B. Davies, A. Evers, L. Johansson, M. Knapen, M. Thorslund and C. Tunisse *Care for the Elderly – Significant Innovations in Three European Countries*. Frankfurt: Campus/Westview. 1–6.

Finch, J. (1984) 'Community care: developing non-sexist alternatives.' *Critial Social Policy 9*, 6–18.

Finch, J. and Groves, D. (1980) 'Community care and the family: a case for equal opportunities?.' *Journal of Social Policy 9*, 4, 487–514.

Fisher, M. (ed) (1989) *Client Studies*. Sheffield: JUSSR.

Friedmann, R., Gilbert, N. and Sherer, M. (eds) (1987) *Modern Welfare States*. Hemel Hempstead: Wheatsheaf.

Henwood, M. and Wicks, M. (1984) *The Forgotten Army: Family Care and Elderly People*. London: Family Policy Studies Centre.

Jamieson, A. (ed) (1991) *Home Care for Older People in Europe*. Oxford: OUP.

Jamieson, A. and Illsley, R. (eds) (1990) *Contrasting European Policies for the Care of Older People*. Aldershot: Avebury.

Kraan, R.J., Baldock, J., Davies, B., Evers, A., Johansson, L., Knapen, M., Thorslund, M. and Tunissen, C. (1991) *Care for the Elderly – Significant Innovations in Three European Countries*. Frankfurt: Campus/Westview.

Land, H. (1978) 'Who cares for the family?' *Journal of Social Policy 7*, 3, 357–84.

Levin, E., Sinclair, I. and Gorbach, P. (1985) 'The effectiveness of the home help service with confused old people and their families.' *Research, Policy and Planning 3*, 2, 1–7.

Mayer, J. and Timms, N. (1970) *The Client Speaks*. London: Routledge.

Nijkamp, P., Pacolet, J., Spinnewyn, H., Vollering, A., Wilderom, C. and Winters, S. (1991) *Services for the Elderly in Europe*. Leuven: HIVA.

Oliver, J. (1983) 'The caring wife.' In J. Finch and D. Groves (eds) *A Labour of Love: Women, Work and Caring.* London: Routledge and Kegan Paul, 72–78.

Pacolet, J., Versieck, K. and Bouten, R. (1994) *Social Protection for Dependency in Old Age.* Leuven: Hoger Institute.

Phillipson, C. and Walker, A. (eds) (1986) *Ageing and Social Policy.* Aldershot: Gower.

Qureshi, H. and Walker, A. (1989) *The Caring Relationship.* London: Macmillan.

Sainsbury, E. (1980) 'Client need, social work method and agency function: a research perspective.' *Social Work Service 23*, 9–15.

Twigg, J., Atkin, K. and Perring, C. (1990) *Carers and Services: A Review of Research.* London: HMSO.

Waerness, K. (1986) 'Informal and formal care in old age?' Paper presented to the XIth World Congress of Sociology, New Delhi.

Waerness, K. (1990) 'What can a promotive orientation of health and care services mean for women as professionals and family carers?' Paper No. 8, Vienna Dialogue V, European Centre.

Walker, A. (1981) 'Community care and the elderly in Great Britain: theory and practice.' *International Journal of Health Services 11*, 4, 541–57.

Walker, A. (1985) *The Care Gap.* London: Local Government Information Unit.

Walker, A. (1989) 'Community care.' In M. McCarthy (ed) *The New Politics of Welfare.* London: Macmillan, 203–224.

Walker, A. (1990) 'The economic "burden" of ageing and the prospect of intergenerational conflict.' *Ageing and Society 10*, 2, 377–396.

Walker, A. (1992) 'Increasing user involvement in the Social Services.' In T. Arie (ed) *Recent Advances in Psychogeriatrics 2.* London: Churchill Livingstone, 5–19.

Walker, A. (1993a) *Age and Attitudes.* Brussels: Commission of the EC.

Walker, A. (1993b) 'Intergenerational relations and welfare restructuring: The social construction of an intergenerational Problem.' In V. Bengston and W.A. Achenbaum (eds) *The Changing Contract Across the Generations.* New York: Aldine, 141–165.

Walker, A., Alber, J. and Guillemard, A-M. (1993) *Older People in Europe: Social and Economic Policies.* Brussels: Commission of the EC.

Walker, A., Guillemard, A-M. and Alber, J. (1991) *Social and Economic Policies and Older People*. Brussels: Commission of the European Communities.

Warren, L. (1990) '"We're Home Helps because we care": The experience of Home Helps caring for elderly people.' In P. Abbot and G. Payne (eds) *New Directions in the Sociology of Health*. Basingstoke: Falmer Press, 70–86.

Wright, F. (1986) *Left to Care Alone*. Aldershot: Gower.

Part II

Adopting a User- and Carer-Led Approach to Services

Chapter 5

New Perspectives on Housing and Support for Older People

Bridget J. Franklin

This chapter examines the crucial role that housing plays in the lives of older people, as it does in the lives of people of all ages, and its hitherto relative neglect in terms of community care planning and implementation.

> 'The Government believes that housing is a vital component of community care and it is often the key to independent living.' (Cmnd 849 1989, para 3.5.1)

Concerns about the lack of a robust framework for the housing dimension of community care were voiced after the publication of the Griffiths report *Community Care: Agenda for Action* (1988). Griffiths had maintained that the responsibility of housing authorities should be solely concerned with the 'bricks and mortar', and that social service departments should be responsible for any functions which had a welfare or caring element. Griffiths has been widely criticised for underestimating the significance of housing in people's lives and the importance of housing as the base to which services are delivered, and for misunderstanding the potential for housing staff to operate as part of a multi-disciplinary team. The White Paper *Caring for People* states:

> 'Social services authorities will need to work closely with housing authorities, housing associations and other providers of housing of all types in developing plans for a full and flexible range of housing. *Where necessary*, housing needs should form part of an assessment of care needs...' (Cmnd 849 1989, para 3.54 (italics added))

This relegation of housing to an insignificant afterthought has much more serious implications than merely the lack of involvement of housing agencies in community care planning and community care assessments. The denial of the centrality of housing in people's lives and the perpetuation of certain myths and stereotypes serve to obstruct new responses. The need for housing has usually been given a narrow interpretation in terms of the provision of shelter from the elements, and the maintenance of physical health. It is this narrow interpretation which is at the heart of state housing policies and which is in danger of being perpetuated in the context of community care.

In the past the response of the State to the perceived needs of those with a disadvantage or disability has all too often been to remove them from their existing environment and place them in one occupied by others similarly disadvantaged. Here, physical health may be maintained, but autonomy and self-expression are sacrificed to a regime of surveillance and strict routine. It was in reaction to the disabling effects of institutionalisation that the move to normalisation and ordinary living spread, first from Scandinavia and then from the US. The new emphasis on ordinary housing, while to be welcomed as a policy move, nonetheless has its dangers. To insist on ordinary mainstream housing for all, regardless of condition, can have harmful consequences for those who genuinely cannot cope, even if assisted by a comprehensive package of care and support. Unless offered as a choice, and within certain parameters, it can become as constraining as was the previous reliance on institutionalisation, exhibiting the same denial of the needs of the total person. It is this rigidity of thinking which has led to the stereotyped ways in which housing is conceptualised by both policy makers and professionals who are limited by their inability to look beyond the narrow range of their own experience and training.

There are a number of sources available which discuss the existing range of housing options for older people (e.g. Rolfe, Leather and Mackintosh 1993, Tinker 1994, Clapham, Kemp and Smith 1990, Oldman 1990). However, these have a tendency to reinforce traditional solutions by discussing the options one by one, and focusing on the provision and the process, rather than either the reasons for the adoption of such options, or the experience of the user.

The aim of this chapter is to challenge the traditional way of looking at housing for older people and to stimulate a more holistic and person-centred approach. The focus of the chapter will be on the stereotypical ways in which the dwelling as object has been elaborated by professionals and providers when trying to meet the support needs of older people. The last part of this section discusses how the home or dwelling unit is perceived and experienced by the dweller. Finally, some examples of attempts to achieve more imaginative solutions are given, and recommendations offered for future directions.

The dwelling as structure

In this perspective the home is seen as an envelope which contains the life of the older person. The emphasis is on the manipulation of the physical structure to make the dwelling more comfortable, safe and secure, thus enabling the individual to stay on for longer than might otherwise be possible.

The 1991 English House Condition survey confirmed that older people, and especially older people living alone, occupy the worst private rented and owner occupied housing (DoE 1993). Since this housing tends to be concentrated in urban areas of pre-1919 terraced streets, the question arises as to whether an area, or individual, approach to improvement is more effective. Area programmes such as Housing Action Areas and General Improvement Areas, and more recently Neighbourhood Renewal Areas, have the advantage that not only are individual properties improved, but so also is the general environment. Given that a recent DoE survey into housing attitudes (Hedges and Clemens 1994) has shown that 85 per cent of people consider that being in a good area is as important as having a satisfactory house, this is a not unimportant consideration.

The pros and cons of staying put

However, it is the more targeted approach to home improvement that has become a substantial plank of housing policy for older people, with the explicit aim of enabling them to 'stay-put' rather than 'move-on'. The first 'Staying Put' scheme was established by Anchor Housing Trust to assist older people to stay in their own homes by offering a combination of advice on renovation and repair, assistance with obtaining the necessary finance, and oversight of the performance of the work (Leather and Mackintosh 1992). Its success has led to the introduction of Staying Put projects by other housing associations, and to the establishment of the Care and Repair scheme, which covers a wide area of the country and has government support. The schemes have in common that they claim to place the needs of clients above the needs of the property for repair and improvement. It is this emphasis which distinguishes them from local authority-led improvement schemes, where the main emphasis is on the maintenance of the general housing stock.

At their best, and given committed and informed project staff these schemes do endeavour to address the wider needs of older people who wish to stay in their own homes, offering a range of advice on, for example, benefits and social contacts, as well as addressing the state of repair of the property and supporting the older person through the whole process. However, they are very unevenly distributed across the country. Financing the necessary repair work is often problematic since local authority repair grants are discretionary unless a house is deemed unfit for human habitation, and even then they are means-tested. Given the potential of such schemes within the larger programme of community care it is notable that social services and health authorities are unwilling to lend financial support (Leather and Mackintosh 1992).

In assessing the long-term contribution of Stay-Put projects it appears that of the clients of the original Anchor project a high proportion had moved on within a few years, and that of those who had stayed, a number identified new or ongoing problems, either in relation to the property, or to issues of care and support (Mackintosh and Leather 1992). There are consequently a number of questions about whether some older people might be mistakenly advised to stay put rather than to move on, especially since the majority of those who had moved said it had been a better solution than staying-put.

Aids, adaptations and alarms

The other main way in which the structural dimension of the dwelling is exploited is in regard to aids and adaptations, which themselves are often part of a Stay-Put package. These include ramps, handrails, stair lifts, hoists, downstairs toilets, community alarms etc. Any of these may make a considerable impact on the quality of life of an older person, enhancing and prolonging the ability to cope in the home environment. However, as with the schemes above, the installation of these facilities is hampered by the lack of resources, despite the recent introduction of mandatory disabled facilities grants, and is often subject to delays of months and sometimes years.

Some authorities and agencies have exploited to the full the potential for community alarms. Glasgow City Council for example, where the system is run by special needs officers within the housing department, have installed a highly versatile system. It is technologically sophisticated, acting not only in emergency, but also offering a two way speech system picking up sound over a wide range, an intruder alarm, a smoke alarm, a temperature monitor and a habit monitor. There is no doubt that community alarm systems enhance feelings of security, however, there are slightly worrying overtones about the level of surveillance and loss of privacy involved. This will be even more intrusive if suggestions to monitor more confused older people by electronic tagging are implemented. Other technological innovations such as the development of 'smart homes' promise to revolutionise the ability of older people to run a home (Tinker 1994). The excitement this concept engenders among enthusiasts is understandable, but there may be a price to pay in terms of feelings of isolation and imprisonment, perhaps compounded by lack of comprehension about the scope and operation of the equipment, and anxieties about how to cope should it break down.

Caution should be exercised in promoting structural solutions, since they may neglect the long-term implications and the anxiety both of ongoing maintenance and increasing care and support needs. There is a danger that in order to justify their existence, the agencies which provide such services sacrifice a balanced consideration of the total needs of those they profess to serve.

The dwelling as design

This perspective shares to some degree that of the preceding one, in that it primarily sees the house as a structure. However, rather than looking at the potential for renewal it is concerned with the dwelling unit as architectural expression. It has been more often applied to forms of communal living than to individual homes, but the latter too are appearing on the agenda.

Housing for so-called special needs, and especially for older people, is often the subject of projects for students of architecture, and for architectural competitions. In this respect it ranks alongside schools, office developments, opera houses, and now foyers. This juxtaposition suggests that in design terms the emphasis is on the public and the communal rather than the private and domestic. Dwelling units that are designed in this tradition are more about claims to prestige for individual architects than fulfilling user needs, and are a reflection of an architectural, and not a user-centred, aesthetic. Nonetheless, realisation of the limitations of some of the earlier building types of collective housing for older people has led to real attempts to create environments which are less institutional and on a more domestic scale. In design terms this means that efforts are being made to avoid monotonous corridors by the insertion of alcoves with seating and natural lighting, to position dwelling units and shared facilities in small clusters rather than in undifferentiated blocks, to aid orientation by, for example, colour coding of different floors and functional areas, and to provide intimate outdoor spaces with interesting planting (as illustrated in, for example, Valins 1988, Salmon 1993). It is also suggested that the traditional almshouse idyll of reflection and tranquillity encourages withdrawal and apathy, and that the opportunity to observe (and participate in) scenes of activity and variety may be valuable in stimulating social engagement and psychological well-being (Valins 1988). Another reversal of popular perception has shown that effective sheltered housing does not need to be provided in purposely designed structures. In Glasgow and elsewhere it has been demonstrated that previously unpopular tower blocks can be converted to sheltered housing if combined with appropriate management changes such as the introduction of a 24-hour concierge service.

The design and finish of mainstream housing has remained intrinsically unchanged for decades, although standards have undoubtedly improved. However, increasing emphasis on independent living has focused attention on design innovations to assist the ability to function in the face of a variety of impairments. Such features include electric sockets and light switches at waist height, kitchen units on ratchets which can be raised or lowered, single flight staircases which can more easily accommodate a stair lift, and 'total wet' bath and shower areas. Of more general application is the concept of barrier-free housing, originating in Sweden and the Netherlands, whereby all new and rehabilitated housing has to conform to minimum standards of accessibility for those whose mobility is impaired, including wheelchair users, although not necessarily incorporating full wheelchair housing standards. Both the Housing Corporation in England and Scottish Homes in Scotland are promoting the concept of barrier-free housing.

The Joseph Rowntree Foundation is urging the adoption of design criteria which will produce 'lifetime homes' to a more rigorous standard than the barrier-free concept, and which will contain sufficient flexibility to allow the home to be easily converted to full wheelchair standard housing should the need arise. This includes an identified space within the dwelling which can be used to install a lift. The guiding principle is that such homes can be lived in from infancy to old age, and are as equally appropriate for the needs of a parent managing a pushchair, a teenager rehabilitating from a broken leg, visiting grandparents, as for occupants coping with disability in old age (Joseph Rowntree Foundation, undated).

In a similar way to the structurally-oriented housing interventions discussed above, the housing as design perspective concentrates on the home as physical object, with professionals determining how users should relate to their surroundings. The lifetime homes solution is to some extent as mechanistic as the smart homes concept, and makes the assumption that people should remain where they are rather than move to new, and perhaps more supportive environments. Lawrence (1987) has criticised the proliferation of user needs, design guidelines and model house plans for general needs that have appeared since early this century, arguing that they ignore the personal goals and aspirations of occupants. It seems that the stimulus of innovations in technology and construction is in danger of leading designers to fall into the same trap in assisting people with impairments and disabilities.

The dwelling as economic asset

Housing is an expensive commodity and therefore has a high economic value. To the owner, whether an individual or an organisation, it represents a substantial capital asset, especially if maintained in good repair. It is with this aspect of housing, as an asset, or, on the other hand, as a liability, that this section is concerned.

There are a number of ways in which an older owner-occupier can realise the capital value of a home in order to assist with care and support needs. These include move-on options, such as selling the home to pay for residential care, 'trading down' and thus releasing equity which can be used for other purposes, moving to private luxury sheltered housing; and stay-put options, such as raising a loan on the value of the home to pay for the costs of improvements, or for personal support. There are also a number of mixed tenure options which may enable an older person to buy into a share of a more suitable home than they might otherwise be able to afford. Such shared ownership or leasehold schemes for the elderly (LSE) allow a percentage of a property to be purchased and the rest paid for by rent. Owners can 'staircase up' to a fuller share in the home. There have been suggestions that it should also be possible to 'staircase down' if circumstances change for the worse. These options and their implications are discussed in more detail by Oldman (1990) and Rolfe *et al.* (1993).

In the rented sector older tenants and the properties they inhabit are often seen as a liability. In the private sector many older tenants have been in the same house for years, and consequently rents are low. Landlords may find the returns insufficient to maintain a condition of good repair, even if they are willing to do so. In the public sector, although houses occupied by older people are likely to be in reasonable condition (DoE 1993), there is pressure to vacate under-occupied properties and to encourage tenants to move on – frequently into sheltered housing. There is also often concern among housing managers that if frail older people remain in the general housing stock they will be required (in the absence of social work help) to provide the sort of welfare and support services that detract from the fulfilment of their property management obligations (Clapham and Franklin 1994a).

The decisions and pressures relating to the home as an economic unit can be the subject of much anxiety. These can be aggravated if other family members, concerned with losing their inheritance, or having to support an aged parent in residential care, are drawn into the debate. Since it is easy to fall prey to wrong or partial advice in regard to the home as an asset, it is essential that an older person, especially one who is at all confused, is able to receive sensitive and considered information.

The dwelling as the context for service delivery

In this perspective the actual dwelling is perceived only in so far as it contains features which impinge on the delivery of care services – for example, the need to help a person up awkward stairs, or the frequent assistance needed to keep a coal fire going. The wider environment and significance of the home is ignored.

There are a number of surveys (e.g. OPCS 1994, Allen *et al.* 1992) which demonstrate the extent to which many older people in the community are handicapped by physical or mental frailties. Such surveys fail to make explicit the interaction between these frailties and the environment. However, they do illustrate the extent to which some people become prisoners in their home, unable or unwilling to venture out unaccompanied, their ability to manage domestic tasks and self-care impeded by musculo-skeletal and other disorders. The evidence is that most receive inadequate support services, with one in eight of those needing assistance having no help at all (OPCS 1994). The rigidity with which many social services departments interpret the duties of their home care services emphasises the extent to which they are service and not user led. Cleaning is now on the whole limited to the maintenance of hygiene rather than keeping the home in the good order which is often so important to feelings of well-being. Allen *et al.* (1992) give the example of an old lady who asked the home help to wash the plates on the dresser, but was refused on the grounds that they were ornaments. The same home help refused to shake the front door mat because it was 'outdoor' work.

The sense of imprisonment, lack of dignity and humanity which is engendered by the partial help which is provided is encapsulated in this quotation from the same study:

> 'We need sheltered housing to get out of the eating, sleeping and toileting in the same room. If we had a ground floor flat, he could get to the toilet – and I wouldn't have to empty the commode – and he could get a bath. We could sleep together as well and have a cuddle, rather than being on two settees...' (Allen *et al.* 1992, p.88)

With the emphasis on the contract culture, and the purchase rather than the provision of care services for clients, it is likely that the rigidity of interpretation of care services will increase rather than diminish, further reducing the scope for flexible responses. In addition, reliance on services can induce feelings of dependence and submissiveness which are counterproductive in so-called 'independent' living. It is this perception which has led the Centre for Policy on Ageing (1990) to suggest that environmental improvements should be considered first, as these may be more effective in promoting autonomy.

The dwelling as institution

This perspective promotes the view that the needs of older people are best met in an institutional, or at least communal setting, from sheltered housing to nursing home. It is implied that there is something separate about older people that requires their segregation from the rest of society. To some extent this is a concern for protection; however, this all too easily becomes a desire to control. The place of sheltered housing in the 'continuum of care' has been under question in recent years; its ambiguous position as neither exclusively housing nor exclusively care perhaps becoming a focus of the wider ambiguities about the nature of community care itself. Empirical research has repeatedly shown that it is for the housing element (access, convenience, warmth) rather than the care and support element (warden, communal services, alarm) that residents of sheltered housing have moved (Clapham and Munro 1988, Butler *et al.* 1983, Oldman 1990, Fennell 1987). Many residents are therefore paying for and receiving additional services that they do not need. As Arnold *et al.* (1993) have noted it is a case of people being selected for schemes not according to their needs, but according to their fit with the type of scheme. Significantly, there is now an over-supply of sheltered housing in some parts of this country, particularly of the bed-sit type of accommodation, while those already in this type of accommodation are posing problems for managers and wardens as they become increasingly frail. This rigidity of definition in regard to the level of service in sheltered housing continues as a person moves up the scale of dependency through very sheltered or housing with care schemes, through residential care to nursing home. The increase in physical dependency is paralleled by the lack of control over the environment. This is symbolically represented by a progressive shrinking in the availability of personal space and possessions. The surrender of individual self-expression is symptomatic of the proportional assumption of professional power and control: 'Order is achieved through structuring therapeutic settings, in both their architectural layout and the permissible use of space' (Bartlett 1994, p.192).

The institutional perspective of old age premises that certain levels of incapacity should be assigned to a certain ideal type of caring environment. It is mainly professionals and providers who promote this perspective, motivated by self-interest and a concern to keep control of a territory which defines their sphere of influence. To argue for more flexible and responsive solutions is to challenge such entrenched positions.

The dwelling as lived experience

The past 10 to 15 years have seen the development of a body of literature on the meaning and use of the home, which is both cross-cultural and multi-disciplinary. The aim of such work is to understand the symbolic and emotional significance of the home, and the relationship between the built form, the social order, and the individual. Després (1991) has identified six themes relating to the meaning of the home:

- home as security and control
- home as reflection of one's ideas and values
- home as acting upon and modifying one's dwelling
- home as permanence and continuity
- home as relationship with family and friends
- home as centre of activities
- home as a refuge from the outside world
- home as indicator of personal status
- home as material structure
- home as a place to own.

The longer a person has lived, the more complex and intertwined these signifiers are likely to be, creating a fundamental bond between place and person. In old age the bond is strengthened by a lifetime's experience, the home and its contents becoming a repository of meaning and memories which locate the person in both time and space. It is this element of orientation that may be of particular significance to a person who is becoming confused and demented.

Sixsmith and Sixsmith (1991) in their research into a group of older people in the UK suggest that the interaction between the dwelling and the person in itself acts to sustain independence. The dwelling makes certain demands, either simply because it must be cleaned and maintained, or because mobility within it becomes something of a challenge:

'The home takes on a new role as the place where independence can best be preserved. As independence becomes personally more significant, so does the value that the person places on their home.' (Sixsmith and Sixsmith 1991, p.184)

To ignore the perspective of the dwelling as 'home' and its relationship to a sense of identity, well-being and autonomy is to deny its centrality in human life. However, this does not mean that an individual should be encouraged (or forced) to remain in the home in cases where it is clearly inappropriate, and against the wishes of the older person. But it must be recognised that moving will bring a very real sense of grief, surrender and disorientation, and that in order to minimise this the new environment should contain at least some aspects which compensate for the loss. It is not always easy to unravel which aspect can best serve this need for continuity:

> 'Which are the most salient environmental components of continuity – neighbourhood, house location, house type, furniture, or activities (such as gardening or hobbies or daily walks) – that contribute to positive mental health?' (Cooper Marcus 1992, p.111)

Towards more person-centred approaches

There are encouraging signs that more person-centred approaches are developing, both in the context of ordinary living and in more communal settings. The former involves the delivery of a tailor-made package of support and care to the home, although to be acceptable such solutions must take into account the suitability of the environment and the avoidance of isolation and unnecessary dependence. Models of good practice in this area predate the recent legislation. For example, MacLeod and Smith (1982) describe the home help service in the Western Isles. Here an older person was often able to choose her/his own home help from a list of people already known to them, and then became the sole client of that home help. In this situation the home help became both friend and carer, and moreover the husband of the home help was sometimes found to be assisting in the support role by doing odd jobs and heavy tasks.

In Denmark where measures to separate housing from support have been a policy aim for some years, a more flexible (and free at the point of use) home help service has been developed. Home helpers clean, shop, cook, wash, dress, talk to and go for a walk with their clients, who can receive many short visits within the day, evening or night, either to meet a need, or simply to check that all is well. A training course has been implemented, which can be extended to include further training as a nursing assistant (Gottschalk 1993). This flexible and responsive service, with the potential for one person to provide both support and care, contrasts with the situation most commonly found in the UK, of which the following is representative:

> 'I get the district nurse to come in. Of course she has to come in to do the catheter but she's not the person to help give me a wash down below and help get me into the chair you know – it has to be another person. Now the other person that comes in to get me into the chair is not allowed to wash me...the person who's coming to help me – she can dress me, she can get me out of bed, but she's not allowed to wash me...Oh dear, oh dear, these rules and regulations.' (Zarb 1991, p.198)

Nonetheless, it is clear that the response to the community care legislation has made a significant difference in some areas in enabling imaginative packages of care and support to be assembled to maintain at home people with very severe levels of need. The danger is that these will fall apart due to funding crises, possibly endangering the life of the most vulnerable, for whom no alternative may be available at short notice.

The concept of continuing care delivered within one communal setting is beginning to gain ground in the UK. The aim is to provide a range of facilities on one site which will cater for changing levels of housing, care and support needs. It is still often the case that as people become more frail they have to move within the complex to another unit in order to receive the additional care. This has the effect of emphasising the relentless progress towards death. However, there are new schemes being developed in both the UK and the US which avoid the necessity to move. For example, the Social Services Department in West Glamorgan, in partnership with a housing association, has developed a scheme of flats for 50 older people where extra care can be delivered to tenants who become more frail without their having to move within the scheme, and with no environmental distinction between 'extra care' and ordinary accommodation. However, there is no facility for permanent nursing care (Wertheimer 1993).

An innovative scheme in Sussex has been developed by an independent voluntary organisation under contract to the local health authority, the social services department and local fundholding GPs. Although active older people are not accommodated, the scheme can cater for frail older people through to total incapacity, either in the hospital on the site, or by design adaptation and support provision to existing units. One of the features is a therapeutic garden. A particular innovation of this scheme is the way linkages have been made to the surrounding community, with daycare, laundry services and meals-on-wheels provided to local residents in need, and the use of community-based support staff in the scheme. The architect of the scheme described it thus:

> 'It offers a seamless service where the boundaries between social service, housing provision and medical services are blurred.' (Slavid 1994, p.33)

Anchor Housing Association has also been particularly influential in establishing links between schemes and the surrounding community, by, for example, providing outreach support to enable local people to remain in the community (Social Housing 1993), and extending to local people the facilities of the scheme, from hairdressing and chiropody to financial advice and health sessions (Rawson 1990). However, if it is intended to extend the facilities in this way the effect on residents should be taken into account. For them it may signify the invasion of the privacy of their home and a loss of autonomy over their personal space. For this reason careful attention should be paid to design features which can emphasise a hierarchy of spaces from public to private (Tindale 1992).

In any communal setting it is difficult to provide an individualised service, but even here there is progress. Wertheimer (1993) describes how some schemes are adopting a system of individual care plans which focus on the needs and preferences of residents. In some cases these extend beyond physical care only and include aspects of emotional and personal well-being following the theory of need devised by Maslow (1970). Wertheimer also illustrates how projects which house groups of ethnic elders are becoming aware of the need to provide for the dietary and religious practices of different cultures, which can often require certain design alterations in the home or in communal spaces.

More controversial is the development of an apparently successful independent life care community for 240 over 55s in Staffordshire, conceived and designed by a housing association in close consultation with potential residents. All facilities, including shops and cafes, are provided under one roof, with covered streets, and one main access point served by a reception desk. Extra care and medical facilities are being introduced to cater for the ageing process (Simmons 94). While this may have overtones of an old people's ghetto its success may be more of a reflection of the attitude towards old age and the increasing anxiety about living in an alienating society than to any intrinsic merit of this type of community living.

Conclusion

> 'The old categories are redundant. They are completely out of touch with modern day thinking and modern day demands. The whole field of ageing and the elderly in terms of support care needs to be totally redefined.' (John White cited by Valins 1988, p.5)

The above quotation predates the introduction of the community care legislation and the duty on social services/work departments to provide assessments of need, and construct suitable care packages for all those who require them. It is this new legislation which has created the opportunity in the UK to rethink the whole issue of care, including the housing dimension. As the lead agency, social services/work departments have the potential to be the major players in a redefinition of the community care process, and to weave together the disparate threads that have hitherto resulted in such cobbled and patchy solutions. At present they do not appear to possess the necessary skills base nor the willingness to involve other professionals that are essential to provide flexible solutions that cross the boundaries between health, housing and support (Clapham and Franklin 1994b). All the agencies involved need to relinquish such possessive attitudes, to change their culture and their desire to maintain ownership, and to forge genuine partnerships where decisions about funding and management are taken after, and not before, the needs of the clients are considered (Fletcher 1990). However, as shown above, instances do exist where agencies, or consortia of agencies, have developed innovative schemes which blur the old distinctions between institution and community, segregation and integration, and where the integrity of the individual and the right to choose are valued.

The intention of this chapter has been to stimulate new thinking about the role of housing in the care package, and to demonstrate the multi-faceted way in which it impacts on the social and material world of the individual. To take a constrained view of the dwelling as a design challenge, an economic asset or a place to which services are delivered is to underplay the potential of the home itself to be a vital element in the support of an older person. Similarly, to see the dwelling as only existing in the here and now is to distort the past and future relationship between the home and the person, and to overlook the way in which what was once enabling can become disabling. Traditional responses have not placed at their centre the need to effect a compromise between the different elements discussed in this chapter, but have been biased by the allegiance of the service provider to favour one interpretation at the expense of the others. The need is to move away from solutions which are concerned with containment, protection and risk limitation, towards ones which permit freedom, choice and self-expression. This can be done only by adopting a truly holistic and person-centred approach which seeks to achieve a genuine balance between all aspects of the social and physical environment. The benefit will be not only to society and the generality of older people, but to ourselves as individuals.

References

Allen, I., Hogg, D. and Peace, S. (1992) *Elderly People: Choice, Participation and Satisfaction.* London: Policy Studies Institute.

Arnold, P., Bochel, H., Brodhurst, S. and Page, D. (1993) *Community Care: The Housing Dimension.* York: Joseph Rowntree Foundation.

Bartlett, A. (1994) 'Spatial order and psychiatric disorder.' In M. Parker-Pearson and C. Richards (eds) *Architecture and Order: Approaches to Social Space.* London: Routledge.

Butler, A., Oldman, C. and Greve, J. (1983) *Sheltered Housing for the Elderly: Policy Practice and the Consumer.* London: George Allen and Unwin.

Centre for Policy on Ageing (1990) *Community Life: A Code of Practice for Community Care.* London: Centre for Policy on Ageing.

Clapham, D. and Franklin, B. (1994a) *Housing Management, Community Care and Competitive Tendering: A Good Practice Guide.* Coventry: Chartered Institute of Housing.

Clapham, D. and Franklin, B. (1994b) *The Housing Management Contribution to Community Care.* CHRUS Research Report, University of Glasgow.

Clapham, D., Kemp, P. and Smith, S. *1990 Housing and Social Policy.* Basingstoke: MacMillan.

Clapham, D. and Munro, M. (1988) *A Comparison of Sheltered and Amenity Housing.* Edinburgh: Scottish Office.

Cmnd 849 (1989) *Caring for People: Community Care in the Next Decade and Beyond.* London: HMSO.

Cooper Marcus, C. (1992) 'Environmental memories.' In I. Altman and S. Low *Place Attachment.* New York: Plenum Press.

Department of the Environment (1993) *English House Condition Survey 1991.* London: HMSO.

Després, C. (1991) 'The meaning of home: Literature review and directions for future research and theoretical development.' *Journal of Architectural and Planning Research 8,* 2, 96–115.

Fennell, G. (1987) *A Place of My Own: A Consumer View of Sheltered Housing in Scotland.* Edinburgh: Bield Housing Association.

Fletcher, P. (1990) 'Innovative services and achieving change: Revising the residential assumptions; Making the service fit the need.' In *The Oxford Conference: Supporting Older People in General Needs Housing.* Oxford: Anchor.

Gottschalk, G. (1993) 'Danish case study: modernisation and adaptation of pensioner flats in Copenhagen.' In G. Gottschalk and P. Potter (eds) *Better Housing and Living Conditions for Older People.* Hørsholm: Danish Building Research Institute.

Griffiths, R. (1988) *Community Care: Agenda for Action.* London: HMSO.

Hedges, B. and Clemens, S. (1994) *Housing Attitudes Survey.* London: HMSO.

Joseph Rowntree Foundation (undated) *Lifetime Homes.* York: Joseph Rowntree Foundation.

Lawrence, R. (1987) *Housing, Dwellings and Homes: Design Theory, Research and Practice.* Chichester: John Wiley.

Leather, P. and Mackintosh, S. (1992) Maintaining Home Ownership: the Agency Approach. London: IoH/Longman.

Mackintosh, S. and Leather, P. (1992) *Staying Put Revisited.* Oxford: Anchor Housing Trust.

MacLeod, N. and Smith, M. (1982) 'A model of practice in field care.' In J. Lishman (ed) *Research Highlights in Social Work 3, Developing Services for the Elderly.* Aberdeen: University of Aberdeen.

Maslow, A.H. (1970) *Motivation and Personality* (2nd edition). New York: Harper and Row.

Oldman, C. (1990) *Moving in Old Age: New Directions in Housing Policies.* London: HMSO.

Office of Population Censuses and Surveys (OPCS) (1994) *People Aged 65 and Over.* London: HMSO.

Rawson, D. (1990) *Commercial Enterprises and Sheltered Housing.* Oxford: Anchor Housing Association.

Rolfe, S., Leather, P. and Mackintosh, S. (1993) *Available Options.* Oxford: Anchor Housing Trust.

Salmon, G. (1993) *Caring Environments for Frail Elderly People.* Harlow: Longman.

Sixsmith, A. and Sixsmith, J. (1991) 'Transitions in home experience in later life.' *Journal of Architectural and Planning Research 8*, 3, 181–191.

Simmons, M. (1994) 'Old folks quite at home.' *The Guardian*, 30 November.

Slavid, R. (1994) 'An innovative approach to care.' *Architects Journal*, 27 July.

Social Housing (1993) 'Anchor's Silver Jubilee brings new approach to elderly care.' *Social Housing 15*, 6, 9.

Tindale, P. (1992) *Towards 2000: Designing Housing for Frail Elderly People.* Oxford: Anchor Housing Trust.

Tinker, A. (1994) 'The role of housing policies in the care of elderly people.' In OECD *Caring for Frail Elderly People: New Directions in Care.* Paris: OECD.

Valins, M. (1988) *Housing for Elderly People.* London: Architectural Press.

Wertheimer, A. (1993) *Innovative Older People's Housing Projects.* London: NFHA.

Zarb, G. (1991) 'Creating a supportive environment: meeting the needs of people who are ageing with a disability.' In M. Oliver (ed) *Research Highlights in Social Work 21, Social Work: Disabled People and Disabling Environments.* London: Jessica Kingsley Publishers.

Chapter 6

'I Was Given Options Not Choices'
Involving Older Users and Carers in Assessment and Care Planning

Fiona Myers and Charlotte MacDonald

This chapter explores the reality for service users and their family carers of their involvement in care planning and the extent of the opportunities to exercise choice in how their needs are met.

Central to the rhetoric of community care is the principle of greater user and carer involvement. As articulated in the White Paper *'Caring for People'* (Department of Health 1989), and in subsequent official guidance, the objective is to give users and carers 'a greater individual say in how they live their lives and the services they need to help them to do so' (Department of Health, 1989). Nonetheless, there is what could be called a 'hesitancy' apparent in policy statements. While seeking to redress the balance of power there is, at the same time, a recognition that this shift is not absolute. Unlike consumers of other services, for users and carers, ultimately it is 'the assessing practitioner who is responsible for defining the user's needs' (SSI/SWSG 1991, p.53). Further, the involvement of users and carers in the decision making process is not the same as handing over decision making authority or the resources to act on those decisions.

As a number of commentators have noted, there is a potential contradiction between a policy which seeks to promote consumer choice and participation while also seeking to ration and prioritise resources (Allen, Hogg and Peace 1992, Ellis 1993, Caldock 1994). Lloyd (1991), who analyses this tension in terms of competing 'liberal' and 'conservative' discourses, suggests there is an incompatibility between a 'bottom up' approach emphasising the individual's role in defining their own needs, selecting and controlling the delivery of services and, where necessary, able to seek redress, with a 'top down' approach where 'management' assesses need and allocates scarce and rationed resources.

This tension at the heart of community care policy is not of abstract political or philosophical interest, but makes itself felt at the grassroots level of policy implementation. For frontline workers it can mean, as North (1993) suggests, having to act both as 'neutral advisers' and as 'gatekeepers' to scarce resources. For people seeking support, even if encouraged to participate, the opportunities to act as empowered consumers may be constrained by the limited range of options from which to choose.

Allen *et al.* (1992) found from their study in England, completed immediately prior to the introduction of the new community care procedures, that older people tended to have no choice over what went into their package and that participation was limited to agreeing with what was offered. Given the contradictory nature of the policy, the question this raises is whether, from the accounts of service users and carers, any progress has been made in shifting the balance of power. From interviews undertaken following the implementation of community care, this chapter explores some of the implications of this tension for older service users and informal carers.

The study

The data on which this chapter draws comprise part of a larger Scottish Office funded study being undertaken in four regions in Scotland by the Social Work Research Centre at the University of Stirling. In the course of the study data from a number of different sources are being collected. First, the completion by workers of case monitoring forms for people referred for comprehensive assessment, both at the time of assessment and after a period of nine months (or on case closure), provides information on the social circumstances, identified needs and services provided to 247 people, of whom 144 (58%) are aged over 65 years. Second, interviews with 65 social work department practitioners explored their perspective on the introduction of community care policies and procedures (MacDonald and Myers 1995). Third, users and carers identified through the case monitoring forms, were interviewed about the assessment and care planning process. Follow-up interviews are currently in progress aiming to explore their experience of the implementation of care packages.

The main focus of this chapter will be the responses of the older users and their informal carers, but to set the context it may be useful just to briefly sketch a picture of the practitioners.

The practitioners

Although all the workers in the sample were employed by Social Work Departments, they did not all come from a social work background. Included in the sample were people from nursing, occupational therapy and home care backgrounds, as well as one health visitor and one community alarm organiser. A number of the practitioners had specialist expertise in working with older people. In one region, for example, one worker had been an elderly specialist social worker, another had been a social worker attached to a social work team for older people. But these were in some respects atypical. The majority had previously worked as generic workers, or as specialists in learning disabilities or child care. As a result they were not necessarily experienced in the needs of older people. With the exception of concerns around recognising dementia and the legal implications, this lack of experience was not, however, reflected in their demands for further training.

In terms of their attitudes toward involving users and carers in the process, the majority of practitioners expressed support for greater consumer participation. However, what also became apparent from their comments were the obstacles to realising this goal. Some of these stemmed from the structural constraints within which workers were having to operate, in particular the pre-determined eligibility criteria and the limited options from which to offer people choices. Aspects of practice could also, unwittingly, serve to undermine the involvement of users and carers. For example, workers differed among themselves as to the degree to which they let users and carers see, sign and retain copies of assessment of needs forms and care plans. Third, workers suggested barriers which stemmed from the users and carers themselves, not just communication difficulties, but also difficulties of comprehension on the part of a confused user or someone with dementia. Additionally, workers perceived what they felt was a reluctance on the part of some users to take up the mantle of the informed consumer. Older people in particular were felt to be particularly uncomfortable with the proffered gift of participation. One worker commented,

'For a lot of the older people, part of their need is for someone to do it for them, and not to have the hassle of finding a place for respite or phoning round for care services.'

Other studies suggest that this reliance may be due not to age *per se*, but to the sense of powerlessness on the part of users and carers, and a desire for a knowledgeable and assertive advocate to act on their behalf (Robertson 1993). Meethan and Thomson (1993) also found a tendency for users and carers not only to defer, but to seek to hand over power. This apparent handing over of power may be a positive choice in the way that a 'client' would employ a lawyer or other technical specialist to act as broker, but it may also be an acknowledgement of the asymmetrical power relationships within the welfare market. Workers not only have the knowledge of the market, and the skills to circumnavigate its complexities, but are also keyholders in their own right. As such, users and carers, although encouraged to be partners, may not experience it as a partnership founded on equality.

Users and carers

The users and carers were identified from the case monitoring forms. Workers were asked to approach all the people included in the main study to ask if they were willing to be interviewed. Inevitably with this approach workers will tend to sift out people who they feel would be unable to participate, perhaps because of a communication problem or dementia. People with whom the worker had no further contact or those with whom the worker had a difficult relationship might also be excluded. Identifying an appropriate informal carer may also not be without its problems, as was found in relation to one younger client where the identified 'carer' proved not to be the person caring for the client in the sense of providing physical and personal care. This loss of control over the selection process was, though, balanced by the preservation of the privacy and confidentiality of those users and carers who did not wish to be approached.

A total of 52 users were interviewed, 31 (60%) of whom were aged over 65 years. Of these, over three-quarters were women. Interviews were undertaken with 36 informal carers, 19 of whom were supporting someone aged over 65 years.

Among the carers of older people, four were male and 13 female, the remaining two 'carers' were in fact married couples. In three cases the carer was the husband of the service user, one was the son and one was a sister. The largest group were daughters caring for a parent, comprising 12 of the sample of carers of older people.

In 10 cases the carer only was interviewed because the older person was felt to be unable to participate. In 21 cases the user only was interviewed, and in 9 cases both user and carer were interviewed. Where carers were interviewed it was to obtain their views as carers, not as proxies speaking on behalf of the user.

Where an interview took place with a user and/or a carer, three quarters of the older service users were living in the community, the remainder were in residential care.

Involving users and carers

Terms like 'involvement', 'participation', 'choice' can mean different things to different people. A worker's idea of involving a user may, from the user's point of view, amount to being informed of a decision made elsewhere. In order to conceptualise 'involvement' a number of commentators have drawn the analogy of a ladder (Arnstein 1969, Taylor *et al.* 1992). Although the descriptions of the different intermediary steps on the 'ladder' may vary, essentially they describe the same process of movement from a low level of participation in which decisions are imposed on an individual with little or no discussion of whether, how, where and when support will be made available, through to a high point of service user autonomy in decision-making and resource allocation.

In the context of assessment and care planning, what is at issue is the degree of power or control the user and carer have over the process and its outcomes. Focusing specifically on access to assessment, information sharing and decision making, the aim here is to begin to explore the degree of control and autonomy this sample of older service users and their informal carers appear to be able to exercise over the process. The findings, at this intermediate stage of the project can only be tentative rather than conclusive: raising questions rather than providing answers.

Getting into the system

Not all the service users specifically sought help themselves, or knew who had made the referral. Of the 31 service users interviewed only two had referred themselves to the social work department. Of the remainder, fourteen were unsure who had initially made the referral on their behalf. Carers, on the other hand, appeared to be more proactive with eight of the 19 referring themselves and only two not being aware of the source of the referral.

What is perhaps more important is their understanding of *why* the worker contacted them. Among the sample of users most saw the worker's role in terms of seeing what help they needed. Many identified a change in their own circumstances as triggering the worker's involvement: a substantial number of the users had had falls which had landed them in hospital. But other users cited a gradual deterioration in their ability to cope, or a change in their home circumstances. In several cases these older users were themselves 'carers', and as a result of their own ill-health were less able to provide care. There were also users who recognised that the reasons for the worker's involvement stemmed from their informal carer's inability to continue caring. One, for example, described how the worker came to see her about her going into a home because:

> 'My daughter did not want me in her home...she works most days...(she's) unable to cope with me and her family problems.'

Finally, there were among the service users a few who remained bemused about the worker's involvement. For example, one user who was in a long stay hospital at the time of the interview could not recall the worker being involved at all, and denied that she needed any help. Another service user was unsure who had involved the worker and the reason for the visit:

> 'I was alright, don't know why she came. I think it was just for a chat.'

The carer in this instance referred to her mother's gradual deterioration and the fact that 'you had to go through social work before there would be any placements for care'.

As this example suggests, some carers had very specific ideas as to why a worker became involved, referring to what they perceived as the user's need for residential or nursing home care. Others cited specific types of help they felt they required to assist them to carry on caring. One carer, for example, who made the referral herself, was looking for respite from caring from a demanding parent. Another needed care to be provided while she went into hospital to have an operation. In a number of cases the request for assistance amounted almost to a *cri de coeur*, where a carer felt they could no longer cope with caring.

A recent study describes how much fear can be a motivating force for users and carers (Department of Health 1994), while Meethan and Thomson (1993) describe the relief felt by users and carers on entering into the Scarcroft project. What perhaps should not be overlooked is the possibility that a process which is often set in train at a point of crisis, or when a user or carer is feeling at the end of their tether, or 'like a useless article', may in itself undermine people's sense of their own autonomy, or control over their own destiny.

Exchanging information

Given that users and carers are often, as the seekers of assistance, placed in a dependent position, the onus is much more on the worker to redress this imbalance, both through listening and responding to users' and carers' expressed needs and by providing information.

In Allen *et al.*'s study (1992), just over one half of the older people felt they had had enough discussion about what support and services would be most helpful to them. In the current study users, in general, felt that the worker was listening to them and gave them as much time as they needed, as one remarked:

> 'He let me know he had plenty of time to listen…he was very easy to talk to…I think I discussed all my needs and fears…he's a good listener.'

It could be argued that the apparently high level of satisfaction with workers as people willing to spend time and listen, reflects what Wilson (1993) describes as the public account or socially accepted version, which may be at odds with the private account. However, the responses were not just what Wilson would perhaps describe as 'neutral' polite statements such as 'he's very nice', but quite fulsome praise. One user, for example, described the worker as:

> 'Very kind and helpful, I call her a friend…she has been a brilliant help to me…I think very highly of her.'

Among the respondents, critical comments tended to come not from users but from carers, and tended to be cases where the carer was seeking residential or nursing home care. In several cases, they felt that the worker had listened to them and been prepared to spend time with them, but appeared to be slow to get things moving. In other instances the carers felt the workers involved were too slow to understand the pressure that they, as carers, were under. A number of carers felt constrained from expressing their concerns because the service user was present when the worker came to do the assessment.

What this illustrates is the potential tension between users and carers, and their conflicting perceptions of whose needs the worker should be addressing. This emerged most poignantly in one case where the user wanted to stay living with her daughter but the daughter was seeking a residential placement for her mother. In this case the user felt the worker understood the situation between her and her daughter, but nonetheless 'tried to get me to go to a home. I do not want to go there'. The daughter, for her part, felt that the worker 'would have liked my mother to stay here and have...some day care'. In instances such as these, the worker's role may be that of an arbitrator seeking a compromise solution, rather than the desired solution of either party.

Although the users interviewed indicated that they felt that the worker listened to what they had to say, the comments of the workers suggest that not all users were given a voice. This was found in relation to people with dementia who, although able to express an opinion, were not felt able to make an informed judgement. One worker remarked:

> 'With dementia they don't know what they want and they don't know what's best for them.'

In cases such as these the voice of the carer may not only serve to speak for the user, but also be the loudest in the decision-making process. This is despite, as some workers recognised, the possibility that carers have their own 'agendas'. For users without informal carers the decision-making responsibility may rest solely with the professional. As Fisher (1990) comments, for people deemed unable to make reasoned decisions, 'concepts of choice and participation are nearly meaningless'.

The other side of the coin to being listened to is being informed. Allen *et al.* (1992) found that substantial numbers of both users and carers felt ill-informed about the range of services available. Workers in the current study certainly recognised the importance of enabling people to make *informed* choices. Nonetheless, the comments of the users and carers interviewed suggests that there is a fine line between being 'informed' and being told. In other words, the redistribution of knowledge which would enable the user and/or carer to make these informed choices, may only be partial. One carer, for example, re-marked:

> 'I was given options, not choices. I was told what was available,'

while a user explained:

> 'She told me what I was going to get and I told her what I didn't want.'

Given that knowledge is power, this dependence on the worker can mean that at the point of decision making users and carers are again unequal partners in the negotiation process.

Decision making

Users and carers may feel that they are listened to, but when it comes to having what they say acted upon where does the decision making power lie? Which voice carries the greatest weight and what are the decisions to be made?

The responses suggest that the degree of influence over decisions, if not the power to make them, may be unevenly distributed between users, carers and others. In some cases a medical decision to admit someone to hospital effectively removes the choice of social care op-tions (at least in the short term). Second, as suggested above, there were instances cited by the workers interviewed where the expressed views of the user might be overridden because they were not believed to be based on an informed judgement. In cases where a user continued to prove 'recalcitrant', several workers suggested they might consider invoking the law to ensure compliance. Third, there were cases, evident among the sample of users interviewed, where residential care was being proposed but the users themselves felt the decision was effec-tively out of their hands. One user, for example, felt that she had no choice:

> 'The doctor in the hospital told me I would not manage at home so I had no choice other than to come into this home.'

Fourth, in cases where user and carer disagree, the importance, to a worker, of supporting the carer to continue in their caring role may shift the balance of power toward the carer's preferences, particularly where there is a potential or actual threat of withdrawal of care.

Certainly, several users interviewed felt under pressure to accept residential care because of their informal carer's needs. The comments of some of the carers, however, suggest that they did not always feel that they had any influence. One carer who expected the worker would be instrumental in arranging for her mother to be admitted to residential care appeared resigned to her mother's resistance:

> 'As my mother is not that far gone it is up to her to make her own choice as to what she wants. I agreed. In the end it is nothing to do with me.'

Fifth, of course, is the influence of the worker themselves. Workers are not only advocates and advisers, but also gatekeepers to resources. If a user's or carer's expressed need does not meet local eligibility criteria or agree with the professional's assessment, then professional definitions may prevail. For example, one user interviewed described how he had wanted to move to sheltered housing, but 'the social worker said I was better off where I was'.

Different participants to the process may, therefore, have different degrees of influence over the outcome. But what of the decisions themselves? Users and carers may feel they are a given a good hearing by the worker, but while receptivity to users' and carers' accounts is a necessary pre-condition to consumer involvement, it is not sufficient of itself. Arguably, the touchstone of 'involvement' is the scope which users and carers have to make choices in terms of the needs to be met and the means for meeting those needs. Allen *et al.* (1992) concluded that most of the users and carers in their study had no choices either about what, if anything, went into their package, or about who provided this service and in what way. In so far as consumer choice was exercised it was through refusal or by choosing to discontinue a service. The scarcity of resources was seen by workers, users and carers as putting limits on user/carer decision making powers. Allen *et al.* concluded that 'positive choice among consumers was not really encouraged, and in some cases, was treated as undesirable'.

From the current study, too, it became apparent that, at the point of service provision, for users and carers there can be a number of different levels of decision-making power:

- no opportunity to choose: users and carers are advised what they can have, with only the negative power of refusal (if deemed able to give informed consent);

- opportunity to choose from a limited range of available or pre-determined options;
- opportunity to develop their own package, with the worker acting as broker, or user and carer having delegated authority to make decisions and access to resources.

Levels one and two seem to characterise the experiences of the users and carers interviewed in our study.

Where the decision is between a residential or non-residential care plan, this may ultimately be made by the professional gatekeepers who determine eligibility. One carer, for example, described how the final decision on residential care was 'dependent on a panel vote'.

Among those who had leapt this hurdle, it was clear that even where users were emphatic that they alone had made the decision, it was not necessarily a choice between alternatives. This was either because no alternative was offered, or because of the perceived shortcomings of the only alternatives believed to be available. One service user illustrated this very clearly:

> 'The choice was mine. I chose the home in preference to having the upset of home helps changing…I didn't like the disruption caused when they were changed…sometimes they would be allocated half my usual time. What can they do in half an hour?'

Users and carers did, however, refer to having a choice of homes. But even this could turn out to be more apparent than real, dependent on the availability of places. One user, for example, described how she had been waiting for a place in one home but:

> 'It was made clear to me I would not get a room within (this) home, and I felt I just had to accept this because there was nothing anyone could do.'

Another constraint on 'choice' may be the costs involved both for the users and for the local authority. These interviews with users and carers did not explore charging or their attitudes towards paying for services. These issues are being explored in the follow-up interviews. Workers, however, expressed their concern that people would refuse a service on the basis of cost not lack of need. Thomas (1994) gives some substance to this anxiety in her review of charging policies. But it is not just the cost to the client which may impede choice. Workers were aware that the options available to people being funded by the local authority were constrained by the costs of different resources. One practitioner, referring to residential placements, commented:

> 'The family can look around at the homes. They still have the right of choice provided they are within the financial limits we give them.'

In respect of domiciliary care, too, users and carers would not necessarily experience the process as one of 'choosing', as one remarked:

> 'I didn't choose, you got what was available.'

For some there was some scope for trying out different things, albeit from a limited range. For example, one service user tried meals-on-wheels but did not enjoy the food. The arrangement was changed to a home help coming in daily to prepare and cook meals. Overall, however, the notion that users and carers can pick and choose is undermined by the experience of one carer given the names of five homes for respite care:

> 'Some were far too expensive, some had stopped taking respite, and some were fully booked up.'

There was also little evidence to suggest that users and carers felt able to determine the timing and extent of the service. One service user, for example, remarked:

> 'It would be nice if I could have a longer time of home help. I cannot stretch or bend. The home helps have the inclination, but not the time.'

Nor did their accounts suggest they had much influence over the way the service was provided. One service user was happy to have a home help every day, but would have preferred to have a regular person who would 'know your routine and you would know them'. Another for whom, after some delay, a social carer service became available, commented:

> 'I didn't feel entitled to ask for a type of person who had the same interests as myself.'

The picture which emerges from the comments is of a process whereby the service users and carers agree with what is offered from a fairly standard list of home help, daycare, respite and residential care. As summarised by one service user:

> 'It was decided I would get an extra eight hours home help, I was agreeable to this.'

In general, the respondents did not appear to be encouraged to explore different ways of meeting their needs, nor of being given much scope to choose between means. Their experiences would seem to echo those described by Meethan and Thomson (1993), as decision making between *given* services, rather than greater choice between *possible* services.

While carers seeking residential care for the person they cared for appeared to be more active in asking for what they wanted, on the whole both users and carers appeared to be at a disadvantage in knowing what was available, or possible, or what they were entitled to. As such they were inevitably dependent upon the worker. Furthermore, expectations were limited. Only one user interviewed questioned the level of service she was receiving. Referring to the one and half hour's home help she received each week she remarked, 'But I would have thought I was entitled to more'.

Conclusions

In the context of the assessment, the responses of the users and carers interviewed suggest that they felt they were given a chance by the worker to express their needs, and were listened to. In responding to these expressed needs, however, the comments of the workers as well as of the users and carers imply that different voices carry different weights. The loudest voice may prove to be that of the other professionals and agencies determining need and eligibility.

What also emerges from the responses is the degree of dependence of users and carers on the assessing professional: for support at a time of crisis, for information and for access to resources. It has been argued that for older service users, the ceding of power to a professional may itself be a positive choice. Stevenson and Parsloe (1993), for example, suggest that the concept of 'empowerment' needs to be specifically related to the different material needs of very elderly people, and may need to encompass the older person seeking to hand over tasks which worry them. Along similar lines, Robertson (1993) found that, in recognition of their own powerlessness, older people sought a care manager:

> 'Who had status, who was able to cope with bureaucracy, had good contacts, was shrewd and assertive (with service providers) and could generally ensure the prompt and consistent delivery of the required care.' (p.16)

This approach does pre-suppose that the workers themselves are unfettered by competing demands, but as has been demonstrated (see, for example, Ellis 1993) workers are not only advocates but allocators of scarce resources, using the assessment as a means for rationing demand. In effect, workers too may bring with them other 'agendas'.

As a result of the tension between the competing imperatives of consumer empowerment and management control, people may feel they are listened to and consulted, but, that at the point of decision making, find that the exercise of power is severely constrained. For older service users and the people who support them, there may still be a long way to go on the ladder of participation.

Acknowledgements

The paper draws on data collected as part of a Scottish Office funded study of the Efficiency and Effectiveness in the Delivery of Community Care. The views expressed, however, are those of the authors, and do not reflect those of the funding agency.

The authors would like to thank all those who contributed to the study whether as service users, informal carers or workers.

References

Allen, I., Hogg, D. and Peace, S. (1992) *Elderly People: Choice, Participation and Satisfaction.* London: PSI.

Arnstein, S. (1969) 'A ladder of citizen participation.' *Journal of the American Institute of Planners 35*, 214–24.

Caldock, K. (1994) 'Policy and practice: fundamental considerations in the conceptualization of community care for elderly people.' *Health and Social Care 2*, 133–144.

Department of Health (1989) *Caring for People: Community Care in the Next Decade and Beyond.'* Cm 849. London: HMSO.

Department of Health (1994) *The F Factor: Reasons Why Some Older People Choose Residential Care.* Department of Health.

Ellis, K. (1993) *Squaring the Circle: User and Carer Participation in Needs Assessment.* University of Birmingham: Community Care/Joseph Rowntree Foundation.

Fisher, M. (1990) 'Defining the practice content of care management.' *Social Work and Social Services Review 2*, 3, 204–230.

Lloyd, P. (1991) 'The empowerment of elderly people.' *Journal of Aging Studies 5*, 2, 125–135.

MacDonald, C. and Myers, F. (1995) *Assessment and Care Management: The Practitioner Speaks.* Community Care in Scotland Discussion Paper No 5, Social Work Research Centre, University of Stirling.

Meethan, K. and Thompson, C. (1993) *In Their Own Homes: Incorporating Carers' and Users' Views in Care Management.* University of York: SPRU.

North, N. (1993) 'Empowerment in welfare markets.' *Health and Social Care 1*, 3, 129–137.

Robertson, S. (1993) *Fed and Watered: The Views of Older People on Needs Assessment and Care Management.* Edinburgh: Age Concern Scotland.

Social Services Inspectorate/Social Work Services Group (1991) *Care Management and Assessment: Practitioners' Guide.* London: HMSO.

Stevenson, O. and Parsloe, P. (1993) *Community Care and Empowerment.* York: Joseph Rowntree Foundation.

Taylor, M., Hoyes, L., Lart, R. and Means, R. (1992) *User Empowerment in Community Care: Unravelling the Issues.* Studies in Decentralisation and Quasi Markets, No 11, SAUS, Bristol.

Thomas, M. (1994) *Charging Older People for Care 1993/94 Update.* Edinburgh: Age Concern Scotland.

Wilson, G. (1993) 'Users and providers: different perspectives on community care services.' *Journal of Social Policy 22*, 4, 507–526.

Chapter 7

The Evolution of Daycare Services for People with Dementia

Julie S.M. Curran

Daycare services in the United Kingdom have developed in a piece-meal fashion with little co-ordination between service providers, and great disparity in the level of provision between regions (Tester 1989a,b). *Caring for People* (1989), the Government White Paper outlining community care policy as legislated in the NHS and Community Care Act (1990), emphasises the importance of daycare in enabling older adults to continue living at home and in providing informal caregivers with a regular break.

Daycare services are widely used by people with dementia. A recent survey in three areas in England showed that 67 per cent of a sample of people likely to have dementia regularly attended such services (Levin, Moriarty and Gorbach 1994). The survey also showed that daycare was wanted and appreciated by caregivers and that there was considerable underprovision of service. In this chapter, the potential benefits of daycare for carers and individuals with dementia are described. Current service provision and research on the effectiveness of daycare services are outlined. More innovative models of daycare are given and components of good quality daycare, as identified in a recent Australian study, are summarised. Finally, the implications for policy and practice are discussed.

A frequently quoted definition of daycare is that given by Tester (1989c):

> 'A day care service offers communal care, with paid or voluntary caregivers present, in a setting outside the user's own home. Individuals come or are brought to use the services which are available for at least four hours during the day.' (p.37)

The definition excludes purely educational or social settings. It is an arbitrary definition and may serve to create false boundaries, for example by excluding services providing care for shorter periods of time. However, the definition encompasses most of the daycare services described below.

Potential benefits of daycare services for people with dementia

The basic impairments occurring in dementia include amnesia, disorientation and loss of drive and motivation. As a result of these symptoms, as well as their attempts to adapt to them, people with dementia tend to become socially isolated, to adopt a restricted routine and to stop participating in their favoured interests and activities. Other common sequelae of dementia include poor nutrition, poor hygiene and failure to take prescribed medication. Ideally, people with dementia need support in maintaining as active a life as possible, as close as possible to the lifestyle they would normally have led. Daycare can fulfil a number of functions in strengthening remaining skills and compensating for lost abilities. Activities are an important means of enhancing self-confidence and self-esteem, a way of maintaining cognitive skills as well as a means of assessment and of managing challenging behaviour (Archibald 1990). Daycare services can provide activities which are appropriate to the individual in type and skill level required. The reduction in social isolation through daycare attendance can improve mood and well-being. The provision of meals can help to improve the general health of the person with dementia and prevent the development of diseases associated with dietary deficiencies. Finally, daycare can provide a focus in the life of the person with dementia, a source of pleasure and enjoyment and a place where he or she can feel accepted.

Potential benefits of daycare services for the informal caregiver

Caring for a person with dementia is acknowledged to be a very stressful process, probably more stressful than caring for people with other disabilities (Gilhooly *et al.* 1994). The stress process itself is determined by a number of variables, including the social and economic characteristics of the caregiver, the nature and magnitude of the care required, role strains including inter-personal conflict, individual coping style and the extent of social support (Pearlin *et al.* 1990).

Regular attendance of the person with dementia at daycare gives the carer a regular break. As outlined by Levin and colleagues, it is greatly appreciated by caregivers, a higher value being placed on day care than on other community services (Levin *et al.* 1989). It can foster the caregiver's confidence by linking him or her with professionals who see their relative regularly for considerable lengths of time. In Levin and colleagues' most recent study of caregivers, daycare was the main service giving caregivers of people likely to have dementia a regular weekly break (Levin *et al.* 1994). The break enabled them to carry out everyday activities such as shopping, paying bills, going to the hairdressers and visiting friends. In many cases it was preferred to a sitting service as it provided a longer break and offered more choice over whether to stay at home or go out. In addition, many daycare services have regular carers' groups which are an important source of support. Daycare can thus have an impact on the stress process through reduction in the magnitude of care required, through social support to the carer and perhaps also through enhancing the carer's coping style.

Current models of daycare

Generic day centres for older adults

Local authorities and voluntary or non-profit-making organisations run daycare services in residential homes and, more frequently, in stand-alone day centres for elderly people in general. Of the total number of day centre places available in England and Wales, local authorities provide approximately 77 per cent and voluntary organisations 23 per cent of places per day (Tester 1989b).

Although some people with dementia attend local authority and voluntary day centres, these do not cater specifically for them and include severe dementia, wandering and behaviour problems among important reasons for refusal of admission (Tester 1989b). People with dementia are frequently not accepted by other attenders. In an in-depth study of 14 day centres in Queensland and Victoria, Australia (Davison *et al.* 1994), the authors concluded that people with dementia were often marginalised in generic day centres, participating minimally in activities which were frequently inappropriate to their abilities. In turn, carers were reluctant to leave their relatives when they were not confident that the day centre would be able to cope. The specific needs of people with dementia were not being met mainly because staffing levels were too low and staff frequently lacked the required expertise.

Dementia focused daycare

The specific needs of people with dementia are increasingly being addressed within generic day centres through the provision of day care for people with dementia on separate days or by the allocation of a proportion of the available places to people with dementia. The Dementia Services Development Centre has reported on the Broomhill day centre in Lothian region in Scotland which allocates 20 per cent of places to people with dementia (Lardner, Reed and Suttle 1991). It successfully integrates people with and without dementia for all its activities. Its success is partly due to high staffing levels including a large complement of volunteers, an acknowledgement of the specific needs of people with dementia and the early stage of referral of those people who have dementia so that acceptance by other attenders occurs before memory impairment and other problems related to dementia become very marked.

Dementia-specific day centres

In Scotland there has been a slow expansion in the number of day centres providing care specifically for people with dementia. Run mainly by voluntary organisations, often in borrowed premises, many provide day care only one or two days a week. However, some have their own premises and paid members of staff and can provide daycare for up to seven days a week. This has the potential advantage of avoiding attendance at multiple venues if frequent daycare is required. Staff can build up expertise over time in the management of more challenging behaviour and facilitate good care management through liaison with other service providers in the area. In the recent Australian study of day centres (Davison *et al.* 1994), staff in dementia-specific day centres were more knowledgeable about dementia, better trained and more skilled in the management of challenging behaviour than staff in generic centres. Their attitudes towards people with dementia were more positive and people with dementia were more likely to receive appropriate care. However, the study indicated that day care in generic settings can be appropriate in the earlier stages of dementia when some people may perceive attendance at a day centre specifically for those with dementia as stigmatising and unacceptable.

Day hospitals

Day hospitals are an integral part of most geriatric medical and old age psychiatry services. They are funded by the National Health Service and are staffed by a multi-disciplinary team including doctors, nurses and occupational therapists. While accommodating those who have a dementing illness in addition to physical problems, geriatric medical day hospitals exclude those whose predominant problem relates to their mental state (Tester 1989). In most areas they do not provide significant amounts of daycare to people with dementia.

Day hospitals in old age psychiatry

Most of the daycare specifically for people with dementia in Scotland is provided by old age psychiatry day hospitals (Lardner 1991). The day hospital has a number of short-term functions including assessment, treatment and rehabilitation of older adults with dementing illnesses, depression and a range of other psychiatric disorders. It also has a longer-term role in monitoring and treatment and in the provision of relief to informal caregivers. The latter role evolved at least partly due to the lack of any alternative forms of daycare available. Day hospitals with their staff mix have a clear role in the longer-term support of people with dementia who have more severe behavioural problems or mood disturbance, those who are highly dependent on others and those who have complex physical problems. However, for many people with dementia, longer-term support could be provided closer to home, in smaller, non-clinical settings. There is currently an impetus for a reduction in day hospital provision which has come partly from within the National Health Service (Fasey 1994, Murphy 1994) and partly from the growing recognition among other service providers of the need to provide good quality daycare for people with dementia in as normal a setting as possible. However, there is insufficient provision of appropriate day centres in many, if not most, regions at present.

Effectiveness of daycare services – research findings

The caregiver perspective

It is clear from caregiver reports including those recorded by Levin and colleagues (Levin *et al.* 1989, 1994) that daycare is wanted and greatly appreciated by caregivers, providing a much needed break and enabling them to carry out everyday activities. However, rigorous quantitative research into the effectiveness of daycare services for the caregiver is lacking. Existing studies have focussed mainly on the effectiveness of daycare in relieving psychological stress in the caregiver. In a day hospital study, Gilleard showed that daycare attendance appeared to reduce the level of psychological stress in relatives of a subgroup of patients but that for many carers, daycare appeared to be introduced too late to have any real impact (Gilleard 1987). Wells and colleagues, in a study of relatives of day centre attenders in Australia, found that daycare attendance appeared to achieve only minor reductions in stress levels (Wells *et al.* 1990). Levin and colleagues failed to show any significant reduction in stress levels in a sample of carers of daycare attenders in three regions in England (Levin *et al.* 1989). These and other studies have methodological limitations which prevent any conclusions being drawn on the effectiveness of daycare for the caregiver (Curran, 1995). Nevertheless, there is little doubt that some carers benefit greatly from daycare services. Questions to be answered from future research include the characteristics and circumstances of carers most likely to benefit and the optimal time for the introduction of daycare.

The perspective of the person with dementia
The direct study of the effects of daycare attendance on the person with dementia has been neglected. Existing reports point to improvements in the emotional well-being, social behaviour and cognitive abilities of daycare attenders in up to 53 per cent of cases (Levin *et al.* 1989, 1994, Jones and Munbodh 1982, Wimo *et al.* 1990). In Levin and colleagues' studies, carers, reporting benefits from daycare in 30 to 40 per cent of cases, perceived their relatives as being happier, more relaxed, more confident and talkative and showing more interest in their environment. The full potential of day care in improving the psychological well-being and behaviour of the person with dementia has yet to be examined systematically as these studies all have methodological constraints and any conclusions have to be tentative. Important questions are waiting to be answered on the characteristics of those most likely to benefit and the optimal frequency of attendance. Daycare tends to be introduced late in the course of a dementing illness (Levin *et al.* 1994), too late, perhaps, to have a significant therapeutic effect. Many people receive daycare one or two days a week when more frequent atten-

dance may be required to have a noticeable effect. Many people with dementia attend daycare at more than one site. For some this may limit benefits of attendance by adding to the disorientation of leaving one's own home.

Outcome for the person with dementia has also been examined in terms of the success of daycare in delaying admission to long-term care. Studies carried out to date have been limited in their methodology and no clear answer to this question emerges (Ballinger 1984, Greene and Timbury 1979, Curran, in press).

Components of good quality daycare for people with dementia – an Australian perspective

A recent welcome addition to the sparse literature on quality of care in daycare settings has been the Lincoln Gerontology Centre Australian study of day centres in Queensland and Victoria States. The study used a multi-method, mainly quantitative approach which included direct observation of the general activities of the day centres, interviews with centre co-ordinators and staff, and the completion of facilities inventories. Fourteen day centres were studied and comprised six dementia-specific and eight generic day centres in a variety of settings both metropolitan and rural. Summarised below are some of the key elements of good quality care as identified in the study (Davison, Kendig *et al.* 1994).

Staff attitudes, communication skills and knowledge of dementia

Personal qualities of tolerance, sensitivity and good communication skills were identified as the important characteristics of an effective staff member. Formal qualifications were seen as a requirement for the centre co-ordinator only. In some cases, qualifications were considered to be a disadvantage, fostering a clinical and task-orientated approach to work. Nevertheless, training was seen as crucially important in developing specific knowledge and skills. Training was required to provide staff with a clear understanding of the nature of dementia and associated impairments and knowledge on the management of challenging behaviour. The most important aspect of training was considered to be the fostering of a positive attitude towards professional practice with people with dementia.

In the report, the communication approach was identified as the single most important intervention in caring for people with dementia. The skill lay in knowing when to use a particular approach from a repertoire including validation, reality orientation, non-verbal and verbal cueing, demonstration, guiding, mirroring and touch. Knowledge of the life history of the attender and an accurate assessment of the attender's cognitive functioning and behaviour were perceived as important prerequisites to good communication and care.

Group mix and size

Dementia-specific daycare appeared to meet the needs of people with dementia better than generic daycare. Staff in dementia-specific day centres were better informed about dementia, more skilled in the management of challenging behaviour and more positive about dementia than staff in generic centres. The ideal number of attenders with dementia was seen as ten, larger numbers in either dementia-specific or generic day centre settings causing over-stimulation and contributing to difficult behaviour.

Management and organisational factors

Staff worked more effectively when they had unambiguous job descriptions and when the line of authority was clear. Having a clear statement of aims, particularly if formulated by the staff as a group, gave a clearer sense of purpose, highlighted areas for staff training and was particularly helpful for the orientation of new members of staff. A minimum of one member of staff or volunteer to five attenders with dementia was recommended although this staffing level will be seen as inadequate by many practitioners in the field. Staff support and opportunities to air grievances were considered to be important for the effective functioning of staff (Davison 1994) and it was recommended that shifts should not be longer than five hours.

Facilities

Domestic facilities were found to be most responsive to the needs of people with dementia, with a house setting assisting orientation and participation in domestic activities. Church or municipal halls were seen as least conducive to good care because of lack of facilities and a noisy, over-stimulating environment. Accessible toilets, laundry and bathing facilities, a quiet area for attenders to retreat to if over-stimulated or needing to lie down, and furnishings of a domestic style were all seen as important to good care.

Activities

People with dementia appeared to respond best to individual and small group attention with familiar activities and domestic routines. Successful activities included music, social interaction and reminiscence, meal preparation and gardening. However, activities needed to be individualised and planned in response to personal preferences, interests and capacities. Unsuccessful activities were those which placed unreasonable demands on attenders such as quizzes, crafts, cards and counting games.

Opening times

Centres which were flexible in their operating hours, for example offering respite in the late evening, at night or at weekends, were more responsive to the needs of carers and attenders with dementia as were day centres offering daycare more than two days a week.

Innovations in daycare

The needs of people with dementia and their informal caregivers are very varied. A flexible approach to the provision of daycare is desired if services are to begin to meet these needs. Highlighted below are some of the particular problems associated with daycare and some of the approaches employed to overcome them.

Activities

Larger day centres tend to organise activities in groups with little reference to the preferences of individual attenders. To make activities enjoyable and stimulating to as many attenders as possible an individualised approach is required in the planning stage. This has been achieved at the Holy Corner Tuesday Club in Edinburgh which accommodates eight or nine people with dementia (Goldsmith and Wright 1993). A staff meeting is held once a month and a programme of activities planned for each individual. The individualised approach is enhanced by the high number of trained volunteers present allowing a one-to-one staff-attender ratio.

Other day centres incorporate activities which were habitually carried out by attenders in the past. At Berwickshire Dementia Day Services Day Centre, clients shop for and cook meals for themselves. Other day centres emphasise domestic activities such as ironing, dusting and sweeping in addition to the preparation of meals.

Transport

One of the perenniel problems associated with daycare attendance is the transportation of clients to and from day care services (Levin 1994, Tester 1989d). Most day centres and day hospitals use minibuses and ambulances. Transport problems identified by Tester included limited hours of availability of transport, shortage of specialised vehicles such as tail-lift ambulances and unpredictability of transport arrival times. Variability in the times of arrival and return makes it difficult for carers to plan their day. Long travelling times can be distressing for the client and lead to behaviour disturbance on the bus, travel sickness and rejection of daycare. Some attenders feel stigmatised by having to travel in hospital or day centre vehicles.

Solutions given by Tester included securing an adequate transport budget, a co-ordinated transport system for an area incorporating all the relevant agencies, client groups and venues and the use of volunteer car services and taxis.

The Rosebank day centre in Kilmarnock avoids minibuses altogether by using volunteer drivers with private cars and taxi drivers (Archibald 1992). Use of taxis has allowed more flexibility in the hours of attendance. Because the taxi drivers involved are few in number, they have become familiar with and sensitive to the difficulties of attenders over time. This approach is limited to the more physically fit, however.

The REDS project in Glasgow (Archibald *et al.* 1992), which runs a day centre for up to 18 people with dementia per day, until recently incorporated the bus journey into the activities programme. The escort used the journey for reminiscence work, often focussing on landmarks along the way, and included memory games and songs during the journey.

Daycare as a component of care provided

Daycare can meet only some of the needs of people with dementia and their carers. Some service providers are now trying to meet these needs in a number of different ways which includes daycare. An example of good practice in this respect is Rosebank in Kilmarnock. Based in a local authority residential home, it offers four day places a day, four long-term care and four respite residential places as well as a 24-hour staffed phone line (Archibald 1992). Attenders and carers generally find respite admission to a place already familiar to them more acceptable. The Govan dementia project offers day care for up to 11 attenders seven days a week and has an overnight service with workers checking on vulnerable people at home (Illsley 1992). The day centre also has one bed for crisis care. The REDS project, in addition to day care, offers home support 24 hours a day if necessary and an advice and information service (Archibald *et al.* 1992).

Support of informal caregivers

Most day centres and day hospitals consider carer support to be among their most important roles (Lardner 1991). Most hold regular carer support groups. Some services have tried to address the needs of carers more directly by offering a 24-hour help line, or providing information and advice on dementia and services available. In Strathclyde Region, the Young People's Project, set up to develop services for younger people with dementia, offers a counselling service to carers throughout the region including carers of day centre attenders.

Caregivers who want to come too

Established daycare services sometimes discourage informal caregivers from staying with their relative during daycare attendance. Although most caregivers would not wish to accompany their relative, some are unhappy about leaving the person with dementia at the daycare service particularly in the early stages of attendance. Other caregivers wish not so much for daycare as to have somewhere to go as a couple. Central Regional Council Dementia Initiative tries to accommodate such carers by running a drop-in facility in three towns (Central Regional Council 1994). These provide a relaxed cafe environment where people with dementia and their carers are welcome. Carers can meet others in similar situations and can obtain information on other resources. Alternatively, they can use the facility as a means of respite and take a break for a few hours if they wish. The drop-in facility can serve as a gentle introduction to services and pave the way for the acceptance of other supports. Although this service is not daycare as such, in that it does not provide a formal programme of activities for people with dementia, it illustrates well how other day facilities can have important roles to play in ensuring a comprehensive service. The Dementia Initiative also runs a daycare programme which caregivers are welcome to attend with their relative.

Daycare hours

A problem highlighted by carers in Levin and colleagues' surveys (Levin *et al.*1989, 1994) is the rigidity of attendance times offered by many daycare services. Attendance is usually limited to five or six hours between 9am and 5pm, Monday to Friday. A more flexible pattern of attendance is now provided by some day centres, acknowledging that the routines of carers and people with dementia vary, that daycare may be acceptable at some times of the day but not at others and that care at weekends in addition to or instead of weekday attendance may be required. The approach adopted by Rosebank (Archibald 1992) has been to offer daycare in four hourly units up to 11pm. This approach is facilitated by the use of taxis instead of minibuses.

Home-based daycare

Having a menu of care is now seen as one of the best ways of ensuring that the needs of as many people as possible are accommodated by services on offer. This approach does not have to entail a great deal of extra cost. A recent addition to the menu of care has been the development of daycare based in private family homes. In Central Region in Scotland, daycare is provided in eight private homes each catering for up to six people with dementia (Central Regional Council 1994). The domestic setting enables many attenders to settle in quickly. Because attenders live locally, some walk to the house. The small size of the group facilitates the establishment of friendship and trust. The venture appears to provide good value for money. However, attendance is limited to the physically fit as the private dwellings lack facilities for physically disabled people. It also has the disadvantage of relying on the one or two volunteers who provide the service in each house with the possibility of cancellation if the volunteers cannot attend on the day.

Differing gender needs

Service providers are often aware that the needs of male and female attenders have to be addressed in different ways. While domestic activities and informal chat may suit many women, men tend to prefer activities related to their former employment or hobbies. Alzheimer Scotland Action on Dementia runs daycare exclusively for a group of younger men with dementia one day a week in a community centre in Kilmarnock, Scotland. This appears to meet the needs of attenders very well. The attenders themselves decide on most activities and favour pool, darts, dominoes, indoor bowls, cards and table tennis either in the community centre or in local facilities. Most of the staff are also male.

Younger people with dementia

Most people who develop dementia at an early age, i.e. in their early sixties or before, do not fit easily into available daycare services which cater mainly for elderly adults. Lardner (1991) in a recent survey of specialist day care services for people with dementia in Scotland has noted the dearth of services specifically for people with early onset dementia. Alzheimer Scotland Action on Dementia, which runs day centres for people with dementia throughout Scotland, addresses the problem in a number of ways. Some day centres allocate one day a week specifically for younger people with dementia. In Strathclyde Region, younger people usually attend on days allocated to those in the early stages of dementia of whatever age. In this region, however, sitter services are the more usual source of respite for carers of younger people in the early stages of dementia and are seen as more acceptable to both carers and those with dementia.

Implications for policy and practice

The potential benefits of daycare attendance seem clear from our understanding of the nature of dementia and of the difficulties faced by caregivers. Caregiver accounts emphasise the importance of day care services for them and many people with dementia appear to derive great benefit from attendance.

Further research, both quantitative and qualitative, is required to elucidate for practitioners and policy makers the full benefits of daycare for the person with dementia. Early introduction of good quality daycare could potentially have marked effects on the psychological well-being and cognitive state of the attender, improving their level of independence. The frequency of daycare attendance may be crucial in determining the level of response. The characteristics of those most likely to respond need to be determined. As there is under-provision of daycare services for people with dementia at present and as most people with dementia commence attendance relatively late in the course of their illness (Levin *et al.* 1994), evidence of effectiveness in the earlier stages should be followed by the development of more services to cater for people with less advanced dementia.

Similarly, much remains to be learned about the benefits of day care for the informal caregiver. Daycare services, to be as effective as possible in relieving the burden of care, should be introduced in response to careful needs assessment and in the context of a tailor-made package of care. Daycare will be an inappropriate form of respite for some carers. For example, where a high level of assistance with personal care is required, preparing the person with dementia for daycare may increase workload rather than reduce it (Berry *et al.* 1991) and a sitting service may be more relevant. Previous studies have tended to evaluate day care in isolation, addressing neither the issue of needs assessment nor of other services received (Curran, 1995). There is a need for research to examine services in this context.

For the service provider, a flexible approach to service provision is crucial. Activities should be individualised. The environment should be as homely as possible. Staff need to be clear about their roles and the objectives of the centre. Training in understanding the nature of dementia, an accurate assessment of each attender's cognitive functioning and behaviour and a knowledge of their life history are essential. The rights of attenders to dignity, privacy and respect should be emphasised. Day centres offering extended hours can serve attenders and carers best. Staff should liaise with other service providers to ensure good care management.

Evaluation should occur at day centre level and include the views of staff, caregiver and attender. Eliciting the views of attenders with dementia has not usually occurred in the past but is increasingly recognised as important (Davison, Jordan *et al.* 1994). Staff turnover and sickness rates are important pointers to the quality of the working environment for staff. In-house evaluation through the analysis of critical incidents has been advocated by Davison and colleagues(Davison, Jordan *et al.* 1994). Occasional evaluation by an outside agency is likely to be helpful.

Caring for People (1989) has laid out the principles guiding service providers of community care services. If the rhetoric is to be reality, sufficient resources will have to be allocated to the development of good quality services for people with dementia living at home. Day care services should be provided in response to the assessed need of the person with dementia and the informal caregiver and as part of a tailor-made package of care with due attention to the cost effectiveness of services provided. Co-ordination in the planning of services at a local level is required to avoid gaps in provision and the duplication of services. Flexibility and imagination are required in developing appropriate services in a local context. This includes addressing the needs of minority groups such as younger people with dementia and those from non-English speaking backgrounds.

Day hospitals in old age psychiatry have important assessment and rehabilitative roles but their role in the longer term support of those with dementia needs to be clarified. Because of the staff skill mix and hospital resources available, day hospitals appear to be best placed to continue with the longer term support of those with more severe behavioural problems, mood disturbance, very high levels of dependency or complex physical problems in addition to dementia.

Small dementia-specific day centres in domestic settings with empathic, trained staff and using a normalising approach, appear best placed to provide good quality daycare for many people with dementia. Skilled staff have much to offer in the training of other service providers in the area. However, such care does not require a specific centre but can be provided in private homes and could therefore be developed on a wide scale in rural as well as urban areas. Generic day centres can also cater for people with dementia, either on separate days, or by addressing their particular needs on days of mixed attendance through the organisation of separate groups or the provision of high levels of suitably trained staff. As the needs of people with dementia and their informal caregivers are so varied it is important to have a range of services to choose from, although services ought to be defined by the characteristics of the locality and will inevitably be limited by financial constraints.

References

Archibald, C. (1990) *Activities.* Stirling: Dementia Services Development Centre, University of Stirling.

Archibald, C. (1992) *Rosebank.* Stirling: Dementia Services Development Centre, University of Stirling.

Archibald, C., Bell N., Boyd L., Hunter W. and McClure E. (1992) *Re-evaluation of Dementia Sufferer's Project: A Community Based Multi-Service Project.* Stirling: Dementia Services Development Centre, University of Stirling.

Ballinger, B.R. (1984) 'The effects of opening a geriatric psychiatry day hospital.' *Acta Psychiatrica Scandinavica 70*, 400–403.

Berry, G.L., Zarit S.H. and Rabatin V.X. (1991) 'Caregiver activity on respite and non-respite days: a comparison of two service approaches.' *Gerontologist 31*, 6, 830–835.

Central Regional Council – Social Work Department (1994) *Just Two Days Fishing.* Stirling: Third Report of Project Worker – Dementia Initiative.

Curran, J.S.M. (1995) 'Current provision and effectiveness of day care services for people with dementia.' Reviews in *Clinical Gerontology 5*, 313–320.

Davison, B., Kendig, H., Jordan, F. (1994) 'Approaches to practice and recommendations.' In F. Jordan and H. Kendig (eds) *Quality Day Care for People with Dementia.* Melbourne: Lincoln Gerontology Centre for Education and Research, La Trobe University.

Davison, B., Jordan, F., Tippett, V. and Kendig, H. (1994) 'Quality of care.' In F. Jordan F. and H. Kendig (eds) *Quality Day Care for People with Dementia.* Melbourne: Lincoln Gerontology Centre for Education and Research, La Trobe University.

Davison, B. (1994) 'Human resource management.' In F. Jordan and H. Kendig (eds) *Quality Day Care for People with Dementia.* Melbourne: Lincoln Gerontology Centre for Education and Research, La Trobe University.

Department of Health (1989) *Caring for People: Community Care in the Next Decade and Beyond.* Cm 849. London: HMSO.

Fasey, C. (1994) 'The day hospital in old age psychiatry: the case against.' *International Journal of Geriatric Psychiatry 9*, 519–523.

Gilhooly, M.L.M., Sweeting H.N., Whittick J.E. and McKee K. (1994) 'Family care of the dementing elderly.' *International Review of Psychiatry 6*, 29–40.

Gilleard, C.J. (1987) 'Influence of emotional distress among supporters on the outcome of psychogeriatric day care.' *British Journal of Psychiatry 150*, 219–223.

Goldsmith, M. and Wright, A.M. (1993) *Holy Corner Tuesday Club.* Stirling: Dementia Services Development Centre, University of Stirling.

Greene, J.G. and Timbury, G.C. (1979) 'A geriatric psychiatry day hospital service: a five year review.' *Age and Ageing 8*, 49–53.

House of Commons (1990) *The National Health Service and Community Care Act 1990*. London: HMSO.

Illsley, J. (1992) *Govan Dementia Project Day and Night Care*. Stirling: Dementia Services Development Centre, University of Stirling.

Jones, I.G. and Munbodh, R. (1982) 'An evaluation of a day hospital for the demented elderly.' *Health Bulletin 40*, 10–15.

Lardner, R., Reed, J. and Suttle, D.G. (1991) *Broomhill Day Centre: An Integrated Approach to Day Care for Dementia Sufferers*. Stirling: Dementia Services Development Centre, University of Stirling.

Lardner, R. (1991) *Scottish Specialist Day Care Services for People with Dementia*. Stirling: Dementia Services Development Centre Research Report No.8, University of Stirling.

Levin, E., Sinclair, I. and Gorbach, P. (1989) 'Day care.' In *Families, Services and Confusion in Old Age*. Aldershot: Gower.

Levin E., Moriarty, J. and Gorbach, P. (1994). 'Day Care.' In *Better for the Break*. London: HMSO.

Murphy, E. (1994) 'The day hospital debate.' *International Journal of Geriatric Psychiatry 9*, 517–518.

Pearlin, L.I., Mullan, J.T., Semple, S.J. and Skaff, M.M. (1990) 'Caregiving and the stress process: an overview of concepts and measures.' *Gerontologist 30*, 5, 583–594.

Tester, S. (1989a) 'Identifying the main issues.' In *Caring by Day: A Study of Day Care Services for Older People*. Policy Studies in Ageing No. 8. London: Centre for Policy on Ageing.

Tester, S. (1989b) 'Current provision of day care services.' In *Caring by Day: A Study of Day Care Services for Older People*. Policy Studies in Ageing No. 8. London: Centre for Policy on Ageing.

Tester, S. (1989c) 'Definitions and objectives of day care services.' In *Caring by Day: A Study of Day Care Services for Older People*. Policy Studies in Ageing No. 8. London: Centre for Policy on Ageing.

Tester, S. (1989d) 'Transport and developments.' In *Caring by Day: A Study of Day Care Services for Older People*. Policy Studies in Ageing No. 8. London: Centre for Policy on Ageing.

Wells, Y.D., Jorm, A.F., Jordan, F. and Lefroy, R. (1990) 'Effects on Care-givers of special day care programmes for dementia sufferers.' *Australia and New Zealand Journal of Psychiatry 24*, 82–90.

Wimo, A., Wallin, J., Lundgren, K., Ronnback, E., Asplund, K., Mattson, B. and Krakau, I. (1990) 'Impact of day care on dementia patients – costs, well-being and relatives' views.' *Family Practice 7*, 279–287.

Chapter 8

Evaluating Respite Services

Enid Levin and Jo Moriarty

We aim in this chapter to contribute to the growing debate on how to measure the achievements of community services, using our research on respite care for the purpose (Levin, Moriarty and Gorbach 1994). In the UK, interest in this question has been stimulated by the major changes in the arrangements for social care and the need to assess the impact of the new approaches to service delivery on service users and their family carers (Secretaries of State 1989, National Health Service and Community Care Act 1990).

The aims of social and health care reforms

The overarching aim of these reforms is to enable people to have their needs for care met in their own homes, wherever possible. The policy guidance on their introduction explicitly recognises that family members play a major part in community care, laying upon statutory authorities a responsibility to do all they can to assist and support carers (Department of Health 1990). The provision of such assistance is supported by members of the public, professionals and carers' organisations. There is less agreement, however, about the aims, levels and targeting of support services and the criteria to be used in assessing their effectiveness.

A lack of clarity about aims seems most pronounced when service users have chronic, progressive and unpredictable illnesses such as Alzheimer's Disease and other forms of dementia. Research has shown that the vast majority of people with moderate or severe dementia living at home are cared for by a person in the same household, that one member of the family typically gives far more help with personal care than anyone else and that caring for a person with dementia is more stressful than caring for others (Schneider *et al.* 1993, Levin, Sinclair and Gorbach 1989, O'Connor *et al.* 1990).

The purpose of respite care

Respite, in the form of daycare, sitting and relief care in hospitals, homes and family settings, is a type of support aimed directly at the carers of very dependent people and is expected to assume increasing importance in the context of the policy of community care. However, some researchers (Brodaty and Gresham 1992, Nolan and Grant 1992) have already commented that the emphasis on respite may stem from the supposition that some time off will reduce distress in a carer and that, in turn, this will delay the entry of the person being looked after into permanent residential care. Others, ourselves included, (Levin *et al.* 1989, 1994, O'Connor *et al.* 1991, Wells *et al.* 1990) have suggested that packages of respite are used for three purposes: namely, to support those who want to care in that endeavour, to prepare people gradually for separation and entry into permanent care, and to ration, delay or substitute for residential care. In practice, these aims may often overlap, but clarity about the primary aim of the service to a particular individual or group of carers is required, so that appropriate care plans can be made and the strengths and limitations of the services can be evaluated.

Measuring outcomes: some dilemmas

Descriptive accounts continue to outnumber evaluations of differing approaches to respite. However, a growing number of studies have tackled the complex question of whether community services, counselling and other strategies have detectable effects on outcomes for people with dementia in terms of admission rates to residential care and outcomes for the carers in terms of their mental health. Using these measures, the researchers' results are equivocal and, at best, only limited effects have been reported (Brodaty and Gresham 1989, Harper *et al.* 1993, Liebermann and Kramer 1991, Montgomery and Borgatta 1989, Morris and Morris 1993, O'Connor *et al.* 1991).

These researchers all point out that the various forms of help are valued highly by many carers, that the service inputs are usually modest, compared with the carer's contribution, and that there is scope for expansion and improvements in the services. They emphasise, also, that further work is needed to tackle the difficulties in methodology and hence, in the interpretation of the complex interactions between factors associated with the carer, the person cared for and the services.

Morris and Morris (1993), for example, have suggested that methodological difficulties, such as developing longitudinal measures that can follow carers through different stages of their role and cope with different rates of change, may mean that it is too early to draw firm conclusions on the efficacy of different interventions. They comment that an intervention can be useful without the carer experiencing any change in their emotional well-being or behaviour. Consistent with our own approach in two studies, they suggest that a range of measures at different levels should be employed when looking at the impact of services. The selected measures should enable the researcher to address key questions such as the following. Do the services provide solutions, even partial, to the precise problems faced? Do they meet the needs and preferences of individuals and their carers? Do they address the negative aspects of care-giving? Can they mitigate anxiety and distress? Can they make a positive difference to the carers' daily lives?

This type of approach, while rarely sufficient in itself for the purpose of a full-blown evaluation, adds the important dimension of the individual's and carer's viewpoint. The perspective of service users and their carers is crucial at this point in the evolution of service delivery, as it is congruent with the policy emphasis on putting their needs at the centre of the assessment and care management process. In the rest of this chapter, therefore, we shall present some findings from our research on respite care at the National Institute for Social Work (NISW), drawing out their implications for carers and people with dementia on the one hand, and for those who plan, purchase, provide and evaluate services on the other (Levin *et al.* 1994).

The NISW study

Funded by the Department of Health, our research was undertaken in collaboration with health, social services and voluntary organisations in three areas: a city in the north of England, a city in the south and a rural area in the Midlands. As a first step, in each area the arrangers and providers of respite across these agencies completed forms providing details on each confused person aged 65 or over and living with at least one other person who was using their service on a given date. A random sample of older people and their carers was drawn from the forms completed on 528 people. Two hundred and eighty seven carers and the person whom they looked after were interviewed. About one year later, we established outcomes for the 287 older people in terms of whether they were at home, had died or entered residential care and 243 carers were re-interviewed.

The research provides detailed information on the users of different types and combinations of day, sitting and relief care services and on the carers' experiences and views of the services. It examines the effectiveness of differing mixes of respite in terms of their acceptability to carers and their impact on the carers' mental health and on the elderly people themselves. In the conclusions to *Better for the Break* (1994), the book based on the research, we discuss the scope for developing and improving local respite services.

Although the time span of the study from 1989 to 1991 means that it was completed before the community care reforms were finally implemented, we suggest that the detailed information we collected on care packages, on the carers' preferences and on the practices which they found helpful or unhelpful may be useful to those with a remit to purchase or develop services or to monitor progress towards more responsive, user-led services.

The older people

Given our earlier work, we were not surprised to find that the 287 people in the study formed a very old, highly dependent group. The average age of the people in the sample was 79.1 years and a quarter of them were aged 85–98. Women outnumbered men by a ratio of 3:2. Almost all the men, but less than half the women, were still married.

At first interview, their scores on the Memory and Information Section of the Clifton Assessment Procedures for the Elderly (CAPE) (Pattie and Gilleard 1979) suggested that three in five people were markedly or severely cognitively impaired and a further one in five were moderately impaired. Many of these people had more than one health problem, arthritis being the most frequently reported condition. Using the Behaviour Rating Scale of the CAPE, completed by the carers, to provide an overall rating of degree of dependency, almost three-quarters of the older people were classified as highly or maximally dependent. In the year between interviews, the abilities of most of the older people deteriorated and their carers faced increasing pressure.

Thus, many older people in this group of respite users were as seriously incapacitated as those in residential care.

The carers

The study confirmed that, in practice, it is very close kin who look after people with moderate or severe dementia in the community. The 287 carers were: wives (33%), husbands (24%), daughters (22%), sons (6%), daughters-in-law (6%), siblings (5%), and others (4%). The vast majority (85%) were the spouse or adult child of the person for whom they cared.

Overall, seven in ten carers were women. The mean age of the women was 64, compared with 72 for the men, most of whom were husbands. Forty per cent of the carers reported having a long-standing illness or disability themselves. Yet the amount of help and supervision they provided usually far outstripped that given by other people.

Two-thirds of the carers and older people had lived together for more than 25 years, and most carers wanted this arrangement to continue. As other studies have also shown (Sinclair *et al.* 1990), at first interview, only 11 per cent of the carers said that they would definitely accept residential care if it were offered; by contrast, 61 per cent said they would definitely refuse it.

The carers completed the 28-point General Health Questionnaire (GHQ) (Goldberg and Williams 1988) and the Selfcare(D) (Bird *et al.* 1987) at both interviews, so that we had a means of assessing their mental health and the impact of caring upon it. As indicated by the initial Selfcare(D) scores, 27 per cent of the carers were likely to have a depressive illness. In the case of the GHQ, scores of six or over were recorded for two-fifths of the carers, suggesting they had mental health problems such as anxiety and depression.

Women carers had higher GHQ scores, on average, than men carers. Both men and women with physical disabilities and long-standing illnesses had higher GHQ scores, on average, than others. The combination of factors associated with GHQ scores included: gender of the carer, their physical health and, importantly, the number and nature of the precise problems they faced in caregiving. Thus the higher the level of dependency and the greater the behavioural disturbance in the older people, the higher the carers' GHQ scores.

The carers gave moving accounts of the satisfactions they derived from caregiving. They also spoke of problems, including giving help with personal care, coping with incontinence, having their sleep disturbed, feeling exasperated and leading circumscribed social lives. Once such problems have been identified by thorough assessment, many can be alleviated, if not eliminated, by practical, professional and other forms of help.

Clearly, respite services are relevant to the carers' needs to take a break and to the restrictions on their social life arising from caring. In a typical week, the carers and older people in our sample spent, on average, only 16 hours apart. Half the carers never left their relatives alone in the house and one third thought that they spent too much time together. Ninety per cent felt restricted by caring, half of them very much so. Their reactions to this difficulty varied but most found it bothersome. Against this background, the strengths, limitations and potential of services can be assessed.

The services

In each of the three study areas, a wide range of agencies and professions were involved in purchasing and providing respite. Some of their contributions were unique, some were complementary and others overlapped with or substituted for each other. For example, daycare was obtained through the National Health Service, social services, voluntary organisations and, albeit less often, the private sector. An individual carer's package of respite might be made up of a combination of a visiting sitter from a voluntary organisation, daycare for the older person in a social services day centre and residential relief care in a hospital. This pattern has arisen partly because of the gradual evolution of services over the years with one agency attempting, for example, to fill a gap in local services, to cover a shortfall in the provision of others or to obtain funding for a new development.

Now that the community care reforms have been implemented, social services are required to work jointly with health services and the independent sector to develop locality services and co-ordinate packages of care based on assessment of individual needs. Our study identified the following range of issues which merit the attention of the planners, purchasers and providers of these services.

VARIATION
The capacity of services to assist carers is limited by the level and type of provision available locally. There were major variations across the three areas in the overall resources allocated to respite, in the balance

of the contributions from the different sectors and in the availability of new kinds of services. In consequence, the package of respite which could be arranged for carers in one locality could not necessarily be arranged for those with similar problems in others. For example, while day and residential relief care are available in most areas, sitting and family-based relief care schemes are patchily available within areas and across the country. Sitting services were much more extensive in one area than in the other two. Thus the package of respite and its sources depended partly on where the carer lived.

PACKAGES OF RESPITE

Our sample was made up of 85 per cent of carers using at least one respite service and 15 per cent of carers without respite services. Most carers used a combination of two or three types of respite. Of those with respite, 34 per cent used either daycare or sitting or relief care, 50 per cent used two of these services and 16 per cent used all three of them. Daycare was the main source of a break during the week. Relief care in a home or a hospital was used very infrequently on its own.

The commonest package of respite was daycare combined with relief care. The package including short term residential care was targeted on the carers who showed signs of psychological strain, and on those whose relatives were severely dependent and manifested the highest number of behavioural and interpersonal problems.

Once the carers had accepted respite services, most continued to use them for as long as those they cared for remained at home. Thus the main reason for ceasing to use the services between interviews was that an older person had died or gone into residential care permanently.

While concentrating the more intensive packages of respite on the most severely dependent and behaviourally disturbed people is in accordance with the official policy of targeting 'those in greatest need' (Secretaries of State 1989), it limits the scope for using services to prevent strain in other carers and for giving them some choice about the kind of support they use.

AMOUNT AND TIMING OF SERVICES

A key task for care managers is to construct service packages that are responsive to the individual, differing and changing needs of users and carers. On our evidence, services must change and expand in order to achieve this objective.

Typically, respite services were allocated in standard amounts at standard intervals. Thus, the older people attended daycare once a week, on average, in one area and twice a week in the other two. Overall, carers with sitters were visited once or twice a week, with the sitter spending, on average, three and a half hours per week with the older people. In one area, however, most of those with sitters had a weekly service of over five hours. In each area, regular residential respite was offered to most carers in inflexible blocks of two weeks, with intervals of six, eight or twelve weeks between breaks.

The times of the day and days of the week that services were available were somewhat standard also. Daycare was attended on weekdays between the hours of 10 am and 3.30 pm and very rarely at weekends. Sitters visited in the morning or the afternoon but infrequently in the evenings and, again, rarely on Saturdays or Sundays. Relief care was provided for a fortnight or a week, with the stay beginning and ending on a Saturday. The carers fitted in with the service. They understood that daycare could not be offered in a particular unit on Wednesday if that unit catered for people with dementia on Tuesday only. Some carers would have liked the service at different times of the day or the week and some would have welcomed a more frequent service. Therefore, we suggest that priority should be accorded to expanding and extending these services so that they may respond to the carers' requirements more efficiently.

THE CARERS' VIEWS

The carers' task was unremitting, for people with dementia can be very difficult to live with and very difficult to leave on their own. Carers' opinions on the role of services should be assessed in the context of the limited support available from others.

Consistent with many other studies (Sinclair *et al.* 1990, Twigg, Atkin and Perring 1990), most carers whom we interviewed had relatives and friends who visited, telephoned and gave some practical help; but many did not have anyone who was available and willing to attend to the older person. Less than half the carers said that a relative or friend had looked after the older person for a few hours during the day and only 11 per cent said that someone had taken over from them for 24 hours or longer in the previous year. Many carers, therefore, had to rely on services for a regular break. The strong link between the hours spent at day care and the total number of hours the carer and person cared for were apart from each other highlights the key contribution of services.

In this context, we were not surprised that carers with respite services valued them highly. They identified improvements in their own lives following their acceptance of respite. Indeed, half those with regular daycare or sitter services thought these services greatly improved their lives. Assessing the advantages of daycare, one carer said, 'I'd go mad if I didn't have a day to myself'. Another said of her sitting service once a week, 'It's made a world of difference. It gives me something to look forward to each week'. Evaluating residential respite, a husband said, 'It's taken a lot of worry off my mind now she goes every six weeks'.

The carers were very specific about the kinds of things that respite services enabled them to do. Most mentioned a range of benefits accruing from the service, such as having some time to themselves, being able to visit friends and get on with the chores. Strikingly, essential, everyday tasks such as shopping, paying the bills and going to the hairdressers were the activities mentioned most often. For example, two-thirds of those with daycare and half of those with sitters said that the service enabled them to shop, while the proportion mentioning pursuit of their leisure activities fell in both cases to about one-third.

Most carers using daycare or sitting thought that the person for whom they cared benefited directly from the service also. One daughter thought that her mother benefited from daycare because, 'She seems a lot more alert the next day. She talks a lot more'. A husband said of the sitter's visits, 'It's someone different who will talk to her and listen'.

By contrast, the carers were more divided about the effects of residential respite. Just over 11 per cent reported some deterioration in their relative, increased confusion being the commonest problem. About 40 per cent of carers felt that relief care made no difference to their relative. As one carer put it, 'Nothing changed at all. It was as though he hadn't been away'. Interestingly, a further 30 per cent of carers felt that their relative had benefited from relief care and 10 per cent saw advantages and disadvantages to the stays.

The evaluators of services usually take account of carers' and users' views but do not regard them as sufficient to make the case for providing support. Overall, the carers in our study were very positive about the services. It must be remembered that they were looking after older people who could not manage without their help. We suggest, therefore, that evaluators, as well as assessors, should listen carefully to their views on the benefits of services and take them very seriously. They should pay attention also to their views on the changes that they would like to make in services, for the carers were very aware of the service limitations and identified between them many areas for improvement in practice. Respite, given in standard amounts at standard intervals did not necessarily remove the restrictions imposed by caring. After all, a sitting service for two hours on a Tuesday may be useful in itself but will not enable a carer to continue to play golf with friends available on Wednesday only or to attend a funeral on Friday. A key question is whether the new arrangements for care management will lead to more creative solutions to the precise problems that carers face.

Outcomes

On follow-up of the 287 older people one year later, 46 per cent were living at home, 19 per cent were in residential care and 35 per cent had died. We found it remarkable that 72 per cent of the survivors were still at home.

Our results confirmed the essential contribution of resident carers to community care. First, 7 per cent of the carers had died or entered residential care themselves; only one of the older dependants of this group remained at home, suggesting that the carers were almost always irreplaceable.

Second, of the older people no longer at home, six in ten had died; thus the carers had looked after most of this group until the last weeks or months of their lives.

Third, we undertook a series of multivariate analyses to tease out the factors which most strongly predicted residential outcomes for the older people. We took account of the characteristics of the carers, the older people themselves and their use of various packages of services. These analyses yielded a model of the best combination of factors which between them predicted whether the older people were at home or in residential care at follow-up. In order of their importance, these were:

- the carer's attitude to residential care at first interview
- the older person's level of cognitive disability
- their communication difficulties
- the carer's psychological health

- the older person's age.

Each factor made a contribution to outcome over and above the other variables controlled for. However, the carer's attitude to residential care predicted this outcome on its own and was the most influential of all the predictors considered for the model. Thus, whatever the package of respite used, an older person was very unlikely to enter permanent residential care if their carer would not have accepted it at the first interview.

Finally, we tackled the question of whether services had a detectable impact on the carer's mental health. Our results were consistent with the small but growing number of studies which have shown that the mental health of the carer, as measured by their GHQ scores, improved, on average, if they had ceased to provide day to day care at follow-up, especially if they would have accepted permanent care at first interview (Gilleard 1987, Wells and Jorm 1987, Levin *et al.* 1989). In contrast, the mental health of those continuing to care remained, on average, stable over the year and the direction of the change, if any, was an increase rather than a decrease, in their GHQ scores, irrespective of the characteristics and services examined in the analyses.

Residential care, then, was the service which brought detectable improvements to some carer's mental health, as we had expected. We were not surprised that we were unable to detect similar effects of standard amounts of respite on those still caring. We think that this result should be interpreted in the context of the following considerations. The carers had completed another year of caregiving, one-fifth of them had new psychological symptoms, the abilities of many older people had deteriorated further and the services received had not increased substantially over the year. These carers continued to use respite services and to value them. Moreover, some carers who were not getting respite services at the first interviews had taken them up subsequently. Indeed, in the face of increasing dependency in the older people, many carers said that they could not have coped without them.

Conclusions

We began this chapter by discussing the complexity of the task of evaluating interventions to assist caregivers. We suggested that there is a lack of clarity about the aims of services, especially when users have chronic, progressive illnesses, that the methodologies for assessing effectiveness require refinement and that a range of measures at different levels should be used. In the rest of the chapter, we outlined our approach to evaluating respite services for resident carers and the issues which it has raised. In our conclusions, we shall focus upon those findings with implications for the development and evaluation of support to carers under the new arrangements for community care.

First, we suggest that the role of respite should be assessed in the context of the carers' characteristics and problems and their contribution to community care. We have shown that the carers using respite were looking after a group of very dependent older people, many of whom were as seriously incapacitated as those in residential care. The carers were very close kin, often older themselves, most of whom wanted to continue caring for as long as they were able. On our evidence, their contribution to care was essential and almost always irreplaceable. Their task was unremitting, sometimes very stressful and they faced increasing pressures, as their relatives' illnesses progressed. Each carer was unique and their need to take a break changed over time. Therefore, there was no single type and level of service which would have suited all of them.

Second, when assessing for services, monitoring, reviewing and evaluating packages of care, the views of service users should be heard, respected and given priority. The carers' comments left us in no doubt about the positive effects of respite services on their lives and of their benefits, too, to some of the older people. They valued these services highly, finding them relevant to many, if not all, the problems faced. However, at their current levels, services could only partially remove the restrictions imposed by caring. In our study, an intensive package of respite was made up of day care twice a week, a sitting service once a week, and relief care for a fortnight in every eight weeks. Such packages were targeted on carers who showed signs of great strain and cared for the most heavily dependent people. If we regard services as forming a continuum from permanent residential care at one end to no breaks for carers at the other, then even the relatively intensive packages of respite fall far short of the permanent care end of the continuum, in terms of the break afforded to carers.

Finally, we consider that current levels of provision put limits on the potential contribution of respite services to the support of carers. On our evidence, respite services continue to serve three purposes: first, they are used to ration and postpone the use of permanent care which some carers, albeit a minority, would have preferred; second, they are used to prepare both the carer and the older person gradually for permanent care; and third, they are used to support carers who want to continue to care.

These services do not substitute entirely for permanent care. They are neither very intensive nor very flexible. Given the heavy reliance of the older people on their carers for survival at home, it may be unreasonable to expect that standard services should have a detectable impact on the carers' mental health or prevent entirely the entry of people with moderate or severe dementia into residential care. The carers valued the services highly and many wanted additional support. It may be realistic, therefore, to measure the usefulness of the services by assessing the extent to which they alleviate the precise problems faced by particular groups of older people and carers in particular circumstances. In the UK, the new arrangements for putting service users at the centre of assessment and care management provide an opportunity to offer flexible and responsive solutions to the carers' individual and changing needs, and to test the efficacy of these interventions. The challenge lies in ensuring that services have the resources and standards of practice to meet these requirements.

References

Bird, A.S., Macdonald, A.J.D., Mann A.H. and Philpott, M.P. (1987) 'Preliminary experience with the Selfcare(D): a self-rating depression questionnaire for use in elderly, non-institutionalised subjects.' *International Journal of Geriatric Psychiatry* 2, 830–835.

Brodaty, H. and Gresham, M. (1989) 'Effect of a training programme to reduce stress in carers of people with dementia.' *British Medical Journal* 299, 1375–1379.

Brodaty, H. and Gresham, M. (1992) 'Prescribing residential respite for dementia – effects, side-effects, indications and dosage.' *International Journal of Geriatric Psychiatry* 7, 357–362.

Department of Health (1990) *Community Care in the Next Decade and Beyond.* London: HMSO.

Gilleard, C.J. (1987) 'Influence of emotional distress among supporters on the outcomes of psychogeriatric day care.' *British Journal of Psychiatry* 150, 219–223.

Goldberg, D. and Williams, P. (1988) *A User's Guide to the General Health Questionnaire.* Windsor: NFER-Nelson Publishing Company.

Harper, D.J., Manasse, P.R., James, O. and Newton, J.T. (1993) 'Intervening to reduce distress in caregivers of impaired elderly people: a preliminary evaluation.' *International Journal of Geriatric Psychiatry 8,* 139–145.

Levin, E., Sinclair, I. and Gorbach, P. (1989) *Families, Services and Confusion in Old Age.* Aldershot: Avebury.

Levin, E., Moriarty, J. and Gorbach, P. (1994) *Better for the Break.* London: HMSO.

Liebermann, M. and Kramer, J.H. (1991) 'Factors influencing decisions to institutionalise demented elderly.' *The Gerontologist 31,* 371–374.

Montgomery, R.V.J. and Borgatta, E.F. (1989) 'The effects of alternative support strategies on family caregiving.' *The Gerontologist 29,* 457–464.

Morris, R. G. and Morris, L.W. (1993) 'Psychosocial aspects of caring for people with dementia: conceptual and methodological issues.' In A. Burns (ed) *Ageing and Dementia: A Methodological Approach.* London: Hodder and Stoughton.

Nolan, M. and Grant, G. (1992) *Regular Respite: An Evaluation of a Hospital Bed Rota Scheme for Elderly People.* London: Age Concern.

National Health Service and Community Care Act 1990 Ch. 19 (1990) London: HMSO.

O'Connor, D.W., Pollitt, P.A., Roth, M., Brook, C.P.B. and Reiss, B.B. (1990) 'Problems reported by relatives in a community study of dementia.' *British Journal of Psychiatry 156,* 835–841.

O'Connor, D.W., Pollitt, P.A., Roth, M., Brook, C.P.B. and Reiss, B.B. (1991) 'Does early intervention reduce the number of elderly people with dementia admitted to institutions for long term care?' *British Medical Journal 302,* 871–875.

Pattie, A.H. and Gilleard, C.J. (1979) *Manual of the Clifton Assessment Procedures for the Elderly.* Kent: Hodder and Stoughton.

Schneider, J., Kavannagh, S., Knapp, M., Beacham, J. and Netten, A. (1993) 'Elderly people with advanced cognitive impairment in England: resource use and costs.' *Ageing and Society 13,* 27–50.

Secretaries of State (1989) *Caring for People.* London: HMSO.

Sinclair, I., Parker, R., Leat, D. and Williams, J. (1990) *The Kaleidoscope of Care.* London: HMSO.

Twigg, J., Atkin, K. and Perring, C. (1990) *Carers in the Service System: A Review of Research.* London: HMSO.

Wells, Y.D. and Jorm, A.F. (1987) 'Evaluation of a special nursing home unit for dementia sufferers.' *Australian and New Zealand Journal of Psychiatry 21,* 524–531.

Wells, Y.D., Jorm, A.F., Jordan, F. and Lefroy, R. (1990) 'Effects on care-givers of special day care programmes for dementia sufferers.' *Australian and New Zealand Journal of Psychiatry 21,* 1–9.

Chapter 9

The Needs of Co-Residers
Support for Spouses and Siblings

Gillian Parker

The past 20 years have seen a proliferation of research and comment
on the roles of 'informal carers' – those family members, neighbours
and friends who, by their support and assistance, enable disabled or
frail older people to live in the community. Much of this work has
concentrated on the carers of older people, reflecting national and
international concerns about the growth in the proportion of older
people who live to a great age. Research in this field has tended to
concentrate on the caring activities of the *children*, particularly the
daughters, of older people. To a degree this was driven by a feminist
concern to illuminate the previously taken-for-granted work that
women do in supporting disabled and older people, and by a desire to
question the increasing reliance on women to deliver the objectives of
community care policy (Parker 1993a). This concentration on carers of
a younger generation, however, has meant that caring activity within
the same generation, and particularly that provided by spouses, has
been relatively ignored. Yet, as we shall see below, spouses provide a
great deal of the care that goes to keep elderly people at home, and
siblings are important sources of care for older people who have never
married.

In this chapter we use national statistics to demonstrate the importance of these same generation carers, illustrate their experiences of
caring from the few studies that are available, document the lack of
service support for their activities and raise some questions about the
extent to which support could be improved.

Spouses as carers

Despite their substantial importance as a group of carers, particularly for older people, spouses and partners remain neglected, both in the research literature and in the provision of services.

The numbers of spouse carers

In 1985 the General Household Survey (GHS), a national survey of households in Great Britain, included for the first time questions about the 'special help', or 'regular service or help' that people give to those in their own households or elsewhere because of sickness, disability or old age. The publication of a report based on the data collected provided the first comprehensive national picture of caring activity and carers in Britain (Green 1988). Table 9.1 shows how important spouses are in relation to care for someone in the same household. Indeed, they make up the largest group of co-resident carers. Further, there is little difference in the proportions of male and female carers helping a spouse – 42 per cent and 39 per cent respectively.

Table 9.1: Percentages of carers caring for family members,
relatives and friends by whether the cared-for person lived
inside or outside the carer's household

Relationship to carer	Lives in h/hold %	Lives in other %	All carers h/hld %
Spouse	40	–	12
Child(ren) under 16	10	–	3
Child(ren) 16 or over	12	1	4
Parent(s)	28	45	40
Parent(s)-in-law	9	19	16
Other relative(s)	14	26	23
Friend(s)/neighbour(s)	6	35	26
Base (100%)	727	1743	2470

Source: Green (1988), Table 3.1

If we concentrate only on those caring for older people (women 60 and over, men 65 and over) spouse carers seem somewhat less important. Only 7 per cent of caring relationships for older people involve spouses; by contrast, 50 per cent involve parents or parents-in-law, and 43 per cent 'other' relationships (Parker 1993b). Initially, this seems a rather odd finding, given the importance of spouse carers revealed in smaller scale studies of those caring for older people. For example, Levin, Sinclair and Gorbach (1983) found that 40 per cent of a sample of confused elderly people were supported by their spouses. Similarly, Wenger (1984, p.117) concluded that 'informal carers, particularly elderly spouses, apparently provide the bulk of support for the frail elderly at home' in a rural community. In an urban community, Qureshi and Simons (1987) found that in half of the cases in an elderly population who had an 'identified within-household' helper, this person was a spouse. Reanalysis of the 1980 GHS, which included a special section of questions for older people, showed that more than nine out of ten elderly married people who needed help with domestic and personal care received that help from their spouse (Arber, Gilbert and Evandrou 1988).

There are at least two factors at play here. First, spouses constitute the largest group of carers for older people *living in the same household*. Many of the earlier in-depth studies of caring concentrated on those looking after someone who lived with them. By contrast the GHS included all caring relationships and the majority of these (around three-quarters) were carried out elsewhere than the carer's household. Thus, when we include all caring relationships, the role of spouses is apparently diminished. Second, it may be that the questions asked in the 1985 GHS meant that spouse carers did not identify themselves as readily as others. Perhaps they did not interpret the help or 'looking after' that they did for their spouse as anything out of the ordinary, or did not see their partner as 'sick, handicapped or elderly'. If this latter is the case it has clear implications for care management, and particularly in relation to case finding and assessment.

The fact that older spouses may be under-reporting their caring responsibilities in this way is given credence by findings from the OPCS disability survey carried out in 1985. This shows that 60 per cent of disabled people between the ages of 65 and 74 and 31 per cent over the age of 75 are married or cohabiting. The majority of these (almost nine out of ten) live as a couple with no other adults in the household. This suggests that over 50 per cent of disabled older people are living with only their spouse. Of the older, married disabled people, 23 per cent are severely disabled (in categories 7 to 10 of the OPCS severity scale)

(Martin, White and Meltzer 1989, table 2.3; Martin and White 1988, tables 2.9 and 2.12).

The OPCS disability survey report on informal helpers and carers does not allow us to look in detail at spouses helping older people. However, of the 56 per cent of all disabled adults who received help with activities of daily living, half received this help from their spouse. No other group of helpers was as large. Nineteen per cent of disabled adults had an informal carer – defined as a relative or friend providing assistance with self-care activities. In almost two-thirds of such cases the main carer was a spouse. Further, Table 9.2 shows that 50 per cent of the main carers who were wives and 57 per cent of those who were husbands were over the age of 65. Although there is often a difference in the ages of husbands and wives, it seems a reasonable assumption that the majority of these spouses were caring for older disabled people. In sum, this suggests a level of caring activity among the spouses of older disabled people larger than that indicated by the GHS.

**Table 9.2: Age of carer by relationship
to disabled person (wives and husbands only)**

Carer aged	Relationship of main carer to disabled adult	
	wife	husband
	%	%
<50	16	12
50–64	34	31
65–74	32	30
75+	18	27
All	100	100

Source: Martin, White and Meltzer (1989), Table 8.20

Whether or not spouses make up few of those who care for older people, they are potentially the most vulnerable, as Table 9.3 suggests. As a group they are, not surprisingly, older than other groups of carers. All those looking after older partners in the 1985 GHS were over the age of 45 and the majority (70%) were over the age of 65. Consequently, they were far more likely to be retired. Further, these spouses were among the most heavily involved carers. They were far more likely than other groups of carers to be caring for 20 or more hours a week, to be carrying sole responsibility for caring and to be providing intensive, physical and personal care (Parker 1993b). Thus, while spouse carers may or may not make up a small proportion of those helping older people, it is highly likely that, when they are helping, they are heavily involved.

Spouses are also, for married older people, increasingly the carers of first resort. Studies of the family life of older people carried out in the late 1940s and 1950s suggested that when older men required care their wives were the predominant suppliers, but were often assisted by their daughters who lived nearby. When older women needed care, their daughters were usually the carers of first resort rather than their husbands (Sheldon 1948, Townsend 1957). A number of demographic and social changes appears to have altered this pattern, such that partners of either sex become the carers of first resort when a spouse needs care. Smaller family size or increasing proportions of couples with no children at all, some increases in social and geographical mobility, the increased labour market participation of married women, and, perhaps, changed attitudes towards the desirability of family members' providing care may all have increased the likelihood of spouses' becoming heavily involved in caring for partners, and without the assistance of other family members.

**Table 9.3: Proportions of carers of older people
in different caring relationships who are heavily involved**

Characteristics of caring	Relationship to carer	%
Caring for 20+ hrs per week	spouse	75
	parent/in-law	16
	other	6
Sole carer	spouse	77
	parent/in-law	17
	other	18
Personal and/or physical care	spouse	79
	parent/-in-law	27
	other	16

Source: Parker (1993b), Tables 24, 26 and 27

Being a spouse carer

Most British literature on caring for older people has, until very recently, concentrated on the experiences of adult children, and particularly daughters. Yet as we saw above, spouse carers are important and are likely to be heavily involved. Further, the lack of information about caring within marriage has meant that *men* as carers have been neglected, given that marriage is the prime site of caring experience for them (Parker and Seymour, forthcoming). What, if anything, can the existing literature tell us about the *experience* of caring for a spouse?

Spouse carers experience the same range and types of well-demonstrated effects on their lives as do other carers when, as is usual, they provide care with little support from either formal or informal sources (Parker 1993c). Their ability to take 'time off' from caring is restricted, their social and family networks are truncated. If they have been caring since before pensionable age they will have had their labour market participation and income adversely affected, their expenditure may be higher because of caring, and so on. However, there are differences between spouse carers and others that have their basis in the nature of marriage, which, it can be argued, make the experience *more* difficult for spouses, not less, as some commentators have implied.

First, those whose partners need care earlier than might have been expected – for example with early onset dementia or with physical impairments early in older age – feel that caring for a spouse presents a challenge to 'normal' expectations. This, in itself, is closely related to the nature of the help required, particularly if it involves intimate care. Some commentators have assumed that providing intimate care would be easier within marriage than in other types of caring relationships. For example, it has been asserted that:

> 'the management of disability is smoothed by ageing and the suspension of conventions pertaining to bodily care:…fewer inhibitions ensnare cross-sex help between spouses with personal tasks like bathing and toileting.' (Borsay 1990, p.114)

By contrast, it is claimed, 'Care of elderly parents, and the role reversal entailed, is eased by no such moderating forces' (*ibid.*). However, empirical evidence suggests that this is not so. Some spouses find giving and receiving personal care acutely difficult and that it can interfere with other aspects of their relationship, particularly sexual activity (Parker 1993c). When parents are caring for disabled children, personal care, although it may be more intense or continue for longer than with other children, is, nonetheless, within the 'normal' range of activities for parents. Adult children caring for parents may be able to distance themselves to a degree when carrying out personal care (Lewis and Meredith 1988, Ungerson 1987). By contrast, giving more than a minimum of personal care within marriage challenges many normative expectations. There is no evidence to suggest that ageing does 'smooth' such challenges.

Second, carers may experience caring as more stressful because they feel for their partners; they are hurt to see them in pain or restricted in other ways. As with stressful feelings engendered by giving personal care, spouse carers may be less able than others to distance themselves emotionally from their partner's distress.

> 'This is not totally surprising because being close emotionally is, at least as conventionally portrayed, the main *raison d'être* of marriage. Thus, while we love our children because they are our children and love our parents because they are our parents, by contrast our spouses are our spouses because we love them…even if we stop loving our parents or children they remain, nonetheless, our parents and children. If we no longer love our spouses one of the main reasons for *being* a spouse is removed.' (Parker 1993c, p.119)

The third difference for spouse carers is the combination of physical *and* emotional closeness that helping a spouse entails. Most caring for parents actually takes place in a different household from the carer's, while disabled children attend school, thus giving them and their parents time away from one another. By contrast, the combination of co-residence and the lack of alternative daytime activity for the partner means that close and almost continuous contact is the norm for spouse carers and their partners.

Finally, spouse carers are more likely than others to experience 'role overload'. When caring for an older spouse there is rarely anyone else in the household with whom to share the tasks of caring. Carers may also have to take on the responsibilities that the spouse previously carried. For older women with little experience of household maintenance or older men with little experience of housekeeping, these additional responsibilities can be particularly difficult to manage (Parker 1993c). Spouses may also 'protect' their partners by refusing help from friends, neighbours and even family, thus allowing their partner not to reveal the degree of his or her impairment. This is echoed by American research which shows that older people cared for primarily by their spouses are less likely than others to have 'secondary' carers (Tennstedt, McKinlay and Sullivan 1989).

However, there is also evidence that older spouse carers may not experience caring in such a negative way as do other groups. Wenger (1990) cites a number of studies which, she states, indicate that 'in sound relationships the long history of intimacy in the married relationship results in positive attitudes to caring' (p.199).

Sibling carers

If knowledge about spouse carers is scarce, that about people who are responsible for siblings during old age is even more so. The GHS data fail to distinguish between different sorts of carers classified as 'other' relatives, consequently we have only a limited idea of how important this subgroup may be nationally.

Very few older people live with a sibling, and the proportion seems to be declining with time. So, for example, in 1980, 4 per cent of women aged 65 and over lived with a sibling compared to 3 per cent in 1985 and 2 per cent in 1991. The proportions of men in sibling households were even smaller; 2 per cent, 2 per cent and 1 per cent in the relevant years (Goddard and Savage 1995).

The proportions of older people who live with a sibling seem to increase with age up to 85 and then decrease; in 1991 around 2 per cent of 65 to 79 year-olds were in sibling households, compared with 4 per cent of 80 to 84 year-olds. In the 85 and older age group, however, the proportion dropped back to 2 per cent. The pattern was the same for both men and women, although, as pointed out above, the proportion of men overall in sibling households was lower. However, it is difficult to tease out cohort and life-cycle effects here. The older age groups, particularly the women, are less likely ever to have been married, which may explain why they are more likely to be in sibling households. Alternatively, siblings may become more important as older people lose their partners through death, up to the point at which the siblings themselves die. In fact, both factors seem to be at play here.

The older person's marital status is important; 15 per cent of single men and 16 per cent of single women over the age of 65 live with siblings, as do 2 per cent each of widowed, divorced or separated men and women. By contrast, fewer than 1 per cent of married older people of either sex live in the same household as a sibling.

Even if older people do not live with their siblings they may, nonetheless, look to them for companionship or assistance. Qureshi and Walker (1989, p.53) comment on the dearth of research on sibling relationships in old age and the factors which influence the frequency of contact. Their own research on a community-based sample of older people in Sheffield found that 'siblings were an important source of social contact' although 'frequency of contact...was substantially lower than contact with children' (*ibid.*). Similarly, Wenger (1984) states that the 'importance of brothers and sisters to the elderly may be underestimated' (p.79). Family size in different parts of the country may be important here too. Qureshi and Walker (1989) found that 30 per cent of their sample had living siblings compared with 64 per cent in Wenger's sample.

Given that marital status influences whether or not siblings share a household, it is also likely to be a key factor in the degree to which siblings become involved in care. Both the Sheffield and Welsh studies showed that those people who had never married were in more frequent contact with their brothers and sisters.

Relationships with siblings may also give access to other sources of care. Wenger (1984) suggests that

> 'as time passes...brothers and sisters are less able to support one another and the younger generation takes on the responsibility...More than half the single see a brother or sister most frequently, but nephews/nieces and cousins are approximately three times more important to the single than to the married and widowed combined.' (Wenger 1984, p.88)

Nephews and nieces may thus become an especially significant source of support for older people who have never married or those who are childless.

Widowhood and, to a degree, divorce and separation, seem to have some small effect on contact with siblings but this may be as much to do with advanced age as it is with marital status. Both surveys showed that as people survive longer their contact with siblings tends to increase. Wenger concludes that while part of this effect in her sample is because of the 'higher incidence of singleness and sibling households in the older age group' it is also because 'siblings tend to re-establish or reaffirm ties with their brothers and sisters with increasing age, even where previous relationships have been strained' (p.83). Finch (1989) points to a similar effect where women, in particular, have closer relationships with their sisters in later life, even when those 'relationships had been poor when they were younger' (p.45). This process seems 'to be triggered by the loss of other significant relationships, for example the death of a spouse, or retirement from paid work which removed relationships with workmates and colleagues' (*ibid.*).

All this suggests that sibling relationships may play a small but significant part in the care of older people, particularly for those who have never married. Wenger found that 17 per cent of the older carers in her rural sample were responsible for siblings. However, this relatively high level of help may be related to the rural setting of her study where there was a higher proportion of never married older people than in the population in other areas (Wenger 1990). Other studies, too, have suggested a smaller, but nonetheless important, role for siblings in the care of elderly brothers and sisters (Levin *et al.* 1989).

The impact of higher levels of divorce and separation on sibling relationships and care in the future remains to be studied. On the one hand, there will be more people without spouses who might look to their siblings for support; on the other hand smaller family size means that there will be fewer siblings to look to.

The little that we know about siblings as a source of care tends to be about white older people. However, as Finch (1989) outlines, patterns of immigration and joint household formation may make sibling relationships more important for some ethnic minority communities in Britain, especially in the period of initial settlement. Whether such 'support between siblings may become less significant for the ethnic minority British population in the future' or whether 'the cultural expectations which continue to be endorsed in Britain do embody – for some groups at least – a stronger commitment between siblings than is common in white British culture' remains to be seen (Finch 1989, p.44).

The experience of caring for a sibling

As already stated, there is very little evidence about the experiences of sibling carers. Many seem to take on responsibility for disabled siblings after their parents have died or may acquire responsibilities when siblings become disabled in young adulthood (Hicks 1988, Briggs and Oliver 1985). Hicks calls these 'another smaller but significant group of dutiful daughters' (p.69) who may now be elderly themselves. Such women talk of a sense of being 'stuck with it' – having had no opportunity to negotiate if, how or who should assume responsibility for disabled siblings after the parents' deaths. Often an elder sister simply 'grew' into the role:

> 'It was never discussed, just presumed. I presumed it too, when I made up my mind to come home from abroad.' (Hicks 1988, p.71)

Other siblings presumably become involved in support as their brothers or sisters, whether in the same household or elsewhere, become frail in old age. The degree of involvement will be determined by proximity, other potential helpers in the informal network, and service support. Like other carers, siblings may find themselves providing support at a time of crisis, assuming that this will pass and they will return to their previous level of contact, but gradually discover that their care is required on a long-term basis.

Service responses to spouse and sibling carers

Support for carers has become a major policy and practice issue in recent years, and has been enshrined as a main objective of the new community care arrangements, as outlined in the White Paper, *Caring for People* (DoH 1989). However, there is little evidence that carers who live in the same household as the person being assisted, and particularly spouse carers, are receiving much in the way of support from formal services.

Service response to spouses, who, as we saw earlier, are a heavily involved group, are poor. The 1985 GHS data suggested that few older people cared for by their spouses received mainstream services that might act to help their carers (Table 9.4).

Arber and Ginn (1991) calculate from their reanalysis of the 1985 GHS that some 86 per cent of domestic care tasks for 'severely disabled' older people who were living with their partner were provided by that partner. Only 5 per cent came from formal services and 2 per cent from paid care. By contrast, severely disabled older people who lived alone received 38 per cent of domestic care from formal services and 4 per cent from paid care. A similar disparity in service support for older married couples was evident in relation to personal care.

Table 9.4: Proportions of older cared-for people receiving regular visits at least once a month from professionals or services by relationship

Professional/service	Spouse	Parent/in-law	Other	All
	%	%	%	%
Doctor	16	20	30	24
Nurse	11	14	20	16
Health visitor	4	5	6	6
Social worker	3	5	7	5
Home help	11	23	36	28
Meals-on-wheels	*	6	14	9
Voluntary worker	2	4	5	4
Sheltered housing warden	3	2	2	2
Chiropodist	*	2	2	2
Other visitor	4	4	6	5

* = <1%

Source: Parker 1993b, Table 28

The OPCS disability survey also shows the lack of support that older married disabled people receive. For example, among disabled people aged 65–75 those who were married were only a third as likely as those who were single and living alone to receive home help services or meals-on-wheels. Among the oldest group (75 or over) some 20 per cent of married people received home help services and 5 per cent meals-on-wheels, compared with 46 per cent and 15 per cent respectively for those who were single and living alone. Overall, 56 per cent of single disabled people, over 75 and living alone, received any supportive services, compared with 30 per cent of the single who lived with others and 29 per cent of those who were married (Martin, White and Meltzer 1989, table 4.22).

Data from the 1990 GHS suggest that there will have been little improvement in service support for spouse carers since 1985. Officially published statistics show that levels of service provision to people who live in the same household as their carer have reduced across the board (OPCS 1992).

Nationally available statistics tell us next to nothing about the support offered to siblings who are carers. As already pointed out, the 'other relative' classification in the GHS makes it difficult to tease out siblings from others. However, in some of their analysis, Arber and Ginn (1991) separate out elderly unmarried people who live in the same household, most of whom, they state, are siblings. In such circumstances it seems that, as with spouses, siblings provide the vast bulk of domestic and personal care services to older, severely disabled people, with little assistance from formal services or paid care. However, carers in this group receive somewhat less formal assistance with domestic tasks and slightly more with personal care tasks than do spouses. The differences are accounted for by the involvement of relatives who live outside the 'caring' household.

Much of the reason for the lack of support to both spouse and co-resident sibling carers must lie in the imperative to support older people who live alone. Other things being equal, in circumstances where resources are limited, services will almost always be targeted towards those who have least support from elsewhere. Consequently, any redirection of resources to support carers in substantial ways will necessarily involve difficult decisions about the balance of resources committed between older people who live alone and those who do not.

However, professional attitudes towards different sorts of carers also seem to influence whether or not they receive such support as is available. Professionals and practitioners bring assumptions to their relationships with carers which affect their willingness to intervene in order to provide support, their opinions of different carers as 'deserving' of support, and even whether or not they recognise particular family members as carers (Twigg and Atkin 1994).

This lack of support to spouse and sibling carers is a serious one but not only because of their heavy level of involvement. The American literature suggests that the active involvement of a spouse prevents many older people entering long-term care (Boaz and Muller 1994). Thus, supporting an older spouse who is caring may have positive effects both for the carer and for the partner being cared for.

Conclusions

Spouses are the most important group of co-resident carers for older people and siblings play an important role in relation to older people who have never married. They are among the most heavily involved of carers yet they are also, by virtue of their own age, the most vulnerable. Despite this, service support to these two groups is particularly poor. The attitudes of professionals and practitioners who come into contact with carers are vital in recognising and responding to their needs. However, difficult decisions remain to be made at strategic levels about the extent to which resources *can* be redirected towards older people who have resident carers and away from those who live alone.

References

Arber, S. and Ginn, J. (1991) *Gender and Later Life: a Sociological Analysis of Resources and Restraints.* London: Sage.

Arber, S., Gilbert, N. and Evandrou, M. (1988) 'Gender, household composition and receipt of domiciliary services by disabled people.' *Journal of Social Policy 17*, 2, 153–175.

Boaz, R.F. and Muller, C.F. (1994) 'Predicting the risk of "permanent" nursing home residence: the role of community help as indicated by family helpers and prior living arrangements.' *Health Services Research 29*, 4, 391–414.

Borsay, A. (1990) 'Disability and attitudes to family care in Britain: towards a sociological perspective.' *Disability, Handicap and Society 5*, 2, 107–122.

Briggs, A. and Oliver, J. (1985) *Caring: Experiences of Looking After Disabled Relatives.* London: Routledge and Kegan Paul.

Department of Health (1989) *Caring for People: Community Care in the Next Decade and Beyond.* Cm 849. London: HMSO.

Finch, J. (1989) *Family Obligations and Social Change.* Cambridge: Polity Press.

Goddard, E. and Savage, D. (1995) *1991 General Household Survey: People Aged 65 and Over.* London: HMSO.

Green, H. (1988) *General Household Survey 1985: Informal Carers.* London: HMSO.

Hicks, C. (1988) *Who Cares: Looking After People at Home.* London: Virago.

Levin, E., Sinclair, I. and Gorbach, P. (1983) *The Supporters of Confused Elderly People at Home: Extract from the Main Report.* London: National Institute of Social Work.

Levin, E., Sinclair, I. and Gorbach, P. (1989) *Families, Services and Confusion in Old Age.* Aldershot: Gower.

Lewis, J. and Meredith, B. (1988) *Daughters Who Care: Daughters Caring for Mothers at Home.* London: Routledge and Kegan Paul.

Martin, J. and White, A. (1988) *The Financial Circumstances of Disabled Adults Living in Private Households.* London: HMSO.

Martin, J., White, A. and Meltzer, H. (1989) *Disabled Adults: Services, Transport and Employment.* London: HMSO.

OPCS (1992) *General Household Survey: Carers in 1990.* OPCS Monitor SS 92/2.

Parker, G. (1993a) 'A four way stretch? The politics of disability and caring.' In J. Swain, V. Finkelstein, S. French and M. Oliver, *Disabling Barriers – Enabling Environments.* London: Sage in association with Open University Press.

Parker, G. (1993b) 'Informal care of older people in Great Britain: the 1985 General Household Survey.' In J. Twigg (ed) *Informal Care in Europe.* York: Social Policy Research Unit.

Parker, G. (1993c) *With This Body: Caring and Disability in Marriage.* Buckingham: Open University Press.

Parker, G. and Seymour, J. (forthcoming) 'Male carers in marriage: re-examining the feminist analysis of informal care.' In A. Oakley and J. Popay (eds) *The Trouble With Men.* London: Routledge.

Qureshi, H. and Simons, K. (1987) 'Resources within families: caring for elderly people.' In J. Brannen and G. Wilson (eds) *Give and Take in Families: Studies in Resource Distribution.* London: Allen and Unwin.

Qureshi, H. and Walker, A. (1989) *The Caring Relationship: Elderly People and Their Families.* Basingstoke: Macmillan.

Sheldon, J. H. (1948) *The Social Medicine of Old Age.* London: The Nuffield Foundation/Oxford University Press.

Tennstedt, S., McKinlay, J. and Sullivan, L. (1989) 'Informal care for frail elders: the role of secondary caregivers.' *The Gerontologist 29,* 5, 677–683.

Townsend, P. (1957) *The Family Life of Old People.* London: Routledge and Kegan Paul.

Twigg, J. and Atkin, K. (1994) *Carers Perceived: Policy and Practice in Informal Care.* Buckingham: Open University Press.

Ungerson, C. (1987) *Policy is Personal: Sex, Gender and Informal Care.* London: Tavistock.

Wenger, C. (1984) *The Supportive Network: Coping with Old Age.* London: George Allen and Unwin.

Wenger, C. (1990) 'Elderly carers: the need for appropriate intervention.' *Ageing and Society 10,* 197–219.

Part III

The Practice Context

Chapter 10

Care Manager Co-Location in GP Practices

Effects upon Assessment and Care Management Arrangements for Older People

Brian Hardy, Ian Leedham and Gerald Wistow

Introduction

Both the White Paper *Caring for People* (Secretaries of State 1989) and the subsequent Policy Guidance (Department of Health 1990) emphasised the central importance of General Practioners (GPs) to the implementation of the community care reforms (see Department of Health 1994, for a detailed history). Primary health care teams (PHCTs) in general, and GPs in particular, are uniquely placed within the health and social care service systems by virtue of the extent and frequency of their contact with the general population: 98 per cent of the population is registered with a GP; approximately 70 per cent have been registered with their present GP for over six years; and more than 80 per cent have had contact with their GP during the previous year (Torbet 1990). GPs are widely held to occupy a unique position in public esteem, with no other profession attracting the same trust (Martin 1990). Moreover, they have a 'round-the-clock responsibility for the medical needs of all those living in the community' (BMA 1992, para 2.2). As the first point of contact not only for people with health needs but also, in many cases, those with social needs, GPs have an important 'gatekeeping' role. Furthermore, they are 'in a very strong position to regulate the volume and the type of demand experienced by the social services departments, and to influence the expectations and judgements the public has of local authority performance' (Martin 1990, p.43).

This gatekeeping role comprises the initial identification of social care needs and the referral of cases to social services departments

(SSDs) whose responsibility it is, under the 1990 NHS and Community Care Act, to assess individuals' needs for social care. As we have identified elsewhere (e.g. Leedham and Wistow 1993), SSDs look to GPs for information on problematic medical conditions or disabilities and the effects of these on an individual's daily functioning. Moreover, the requirement for GPs to offer an annual health check to people aged 75 and over is likely to enhance their capacity to identify a wide range of social as well as health needs among this population. Older people, especially those aged 75 and over, are the population most 'at risk' and are also the biggest users of community care services. Most surveys of older people have revealed a 'hidden iceberg' of unmet health and social need (e.g. Bowns, Challis and Tong 1991, Nocon 1993), which points to the necessity for improvements in the initial identification of need and any subsequent assessment. Notwithstanding the debate about the cost-effectiveness of health checks relative to other screening methodologies (see, for example, Nocon 1992, Shackley and Donald 1993) the requirement to offer such checks represents an important opportunity to identify individual needs and, where possible, to feed this into SSD assessment arrangements (e.g. Nocon 1992, Sparkes, Caldicott and Wallace 1993, Department of Health 1994). The likelihood of such information on assessments being shared is clearly enhanced by compatibility between health checks and the SSD's assessment arrangements and also by the proximity of contact between GPs and SSDs. Joint working between these two is thus crucial to the successful implementation of the *Caring for People* reforms. Unfortunately, however, joint working between GPs (or primary health care teams) and SSDs historically has been typified by considerable mutual misunderstanding and even mistrust.

Difficulties of joint working between GP/PHCTs and SSDs

We have reported elsewhere the difficulties that have beset joint working between GP/PHCTs and SSDs (Leedham and Wistow 1993a). These difficulties have been broadly confirmed by a number of subsequent studies (e.g. Hudson 1994, Department of Health 1994), and are summarised below.

Ways of working

Social workers and GPs have different philosophies, training, and language. GPs often criticise SSDs' ability to 'deliver the goods' in terms of a swift response, on demand. In turn, SSD staff criticise what they see as GPs' apparently limited understanding of, or interest in, the needs of the user groups with whom the community care reforms are most concerned; and also their apparent failure to assess the needs of individuals holistically.

Status and autonomy

While GPs not uncommonly characterise social workers as 'amateurish', the latter frequently regard GPs as 'elitist'. In addition, some GPs perceive a tension between their role as the patient's advocate and care management's more explicit rationing processes, fearing that patients who are unsuccessful in receiving SSD services will lose some confidence in their GP. This in turn would strike at the heart of the GP–patient relationship.

Workload and resources

Both the GP Contract and the longer-term shift from institutional to community services and from secondary to primary care have led to concern among GPs that the new assessment arrangements would increase their workload and reduce the quality of their service. In addition, they have been concerned that local government's inadequate and insecure funding bases could make SSDs unable to meet newly-identified needs.

Information and communication

In England and Wales SSDs have found it difficult to relate to a service whose management and representative bodies (Family Health Service Authorities and Local Medical Committees) are unable to require independent practitioners to act in particular ways. Concern has repeatedly been expressed that GPs are poorly informed about the new community care arrangements (e.g. see Birmingham FHSA 1992, Grace 1992, Ivory 1993, 1993a, Millar 1993). Surveys undertaken in March 1993 by *Community Care* and *Doctor* found that 79 per cent of SSDs reported locally-agreed protocols for assessment and care management, while only 17 per cent of GPs thought that such protocols were in place (Ivory 1993a).

Improving joint working: key tasks and service models

We have argued previously (Leedham and Wistow 1993a) that GPs and SSDs should acknowledge such difficulties and that SSDs should seek to:

- clarify and communicate the purposes and benefits of the new arrangements;
- demonstrate practical ways in which GPs can play their part; understand GPs' perceptions and concerns;
- communicate with GPs in ways which maximise the chances of securing their goodwill and active co-operation.

The clear preference of GPs was for consistent working arrangements with someone known to them, who can provide not only quick and easy access and referral but a response which 'delivers the goods'. SSDs have developed three general models to meet these requirements. They can be categorised as: co-location; attachment; and information/awareness about how to liaise with the SSD.

Co-location

The location of SSD personnel in GP practices is a simple and widely attractive idea; and, moreover, a solution long-favoured by GPs. In written evidence to the House of Commons Health Committee (1993) the Audit Commission argued that:

> 'At the operational level, closer working could also be engendered by locating care managers in GP practices, hopefully forging closer links with GPs and the primary health care team. Professionals who know each other personally and who work together should have a much better chance of sorting out the boundary disputes together.' (Written evidence from Audit Commission to House of Commons Health Committee 1993, para 1b, p.2)

In subsequent oral evidence the Commission's Controller, Andrew Foster, said that co-location was 'one of the ways that has eroded some of the negative relationships there can be with GPs because people see a similar role of social care and health care being fulfilled if people work cheek by jowl with each other' (Minutes of evidence: House of Commons Health Committee 1993, para 193).

The benefits of co-location are deemed to flow from its facilitation of team-working and its promotion of greater understanding and trust between professionals, a more co-ordinated approach to meeting needs of individuals and a single access point to a range of health and social care services – the 'one stop shop'. There are a number of examples of co-location projects in England and Wales – Bradford, Northumberland, South Glamorgan and East Sussex, which has run six pilots based in Practices (e.g. Hoddinott, Fordham, Rodrigues and Royston 1992, Royston and Rodrigues 1993) – which attest to the benefits of co-location. The recent Department of Health Special Study on the role of GP/PHCTs argued that improvements were dependent on face-to-face relationships being developed between professionals on a multi-agency basis, particularly between GPs and social workers:

> 'Even the best procedures and agreements appeared to disintegrate or be ignored if they were not supported by the ability of GPs, other PHCT members and local authority staff to resolve potential difficulties through direct contact with each other.' (Department of Health 1994, p.25)

Attachment

Attachment involves a named SSD member of staff providing regular personal contact with a GP practice without being based there. This model has a long history in some areas, and is one which the British Medical Association (BMA) has encouraged (e.g. BMA 1992). The Department of Health Special Study also cites examples of the positive impact of such attachments upon working relationships and communications (Department of Health 1994). The Study made a number of recommendations for linking Care Managers with GPs/PHCTs and underlined that 'the commonly heard pleas from all front line professionals were: "We need a named person" and "We need more contact"' (Department of Health 1994, p.26).

Information/awareness about how to liaise with the SSD

This least structured approach simply involves the provision of information to GP practices about how to liaise with the SSD. Many local authorities have invested in such information and awareness initiatives, most of which involve the provision of a named contact in the SSD; but, unlike attachment schemes, personal contact is minimal or non-existent (e.g. Department of Health 1994).

The Durham Joint Commissioning Project

Background

The Durham Joint Commissioning Project (JCP) originated in a local 'Care Kaleidoscope' simulation exercise in 1991, where the main statutory agencies in County Durham saw the potential for budget-holding care managers and GP Fundholders to work together as equal partners. The Regional Health Authority agreed in 1992 to fund the proposed Project at a cost of £500,000 over two years, part of which (£50,000) was for an independent evaluation – subsequently commissioned from the Nuffield Institute.

The Project proposal argued that 'There is a need to look at new and innovative ways of working at a local level' (Kitt 1992, p.1). The intention was to base care managers initially in two GP practices – in Spennymoor and Darlington – with a primary focus on those people aged 75 and over who were most at risk and who had both health and social care needs. The Project's aim, revised in early 1993 after the Institute's interim evaluation report, was 'to develop joint working practices for the delivery of a unified service that avoids duplication of time, effort, and expenditure, and which is more cost effective and responsive to the needs of users and carers.'

The criteria for selecting particular practices were threefold: to provide 'fertile ground' in terms of likelihood of success; to have one in each of the two health authorities – the South West Durham HA and Darlington HA; and to have one GP fundholding practice, thereby involving all of the potential purchasers, and one non-fundholding practice. The Darlington practice (with eight GPs) was one of seven First Wave (1st April 1991) Fundholding Practices in County Durham, and was thus well established when the Project began. By contrast, the Spennymoor practice (with five GPs) became fundholding six months after the Project began as one of 11 Third Wave (1st April 1993) Practices in the county. The Project was extended to include a third practice – Willington – in order to explore what differences, if any, would result from having only a half-time care manager. The Willington practice was another of the 11 Third Wave Practices that became fundholding on 1st April 1993.

The Project commenced with the appointment of a project manager in September 1992. She initially retained her post in the mainstream social services system, but worked on the Project full-time from April 1994. Two full-time care managers – one for the Darlington practice and one for the Spennymoor practice – were appointed in November 1992 and a half-time assistant care manager was appointed to each practice 18 months later. In February 1993 an Information Systems officer and a secretary were appointed (both full-time). The care manager for the Willington practice was appointed in April 1994 with time allocated equally between the Project and the mainstream social service care management system. Finally, in June 1994 a full-time Welfare Rights officer and a half-time clerk were appointed to serve all three practices during the remaining nine months of the Project.

The study brief

The main aim of the Project evaluation was to assess the impact of locating care managers in GP practices (as integral members of the PHCT) as opposed to elsewhere. The two main research questions, therefore were:

- How did the Joint Commissioning Project model of care management compare with mainstream arrangements within the county and with other models?

- What were the general implications for the development of assessment and care management arrangements?

The principal comparison thus was between the Project system and the newly developing mainstream assessment and care management system. The latter revolve around Customer Services Teams (CSTs) and Specialist Teams. The CSTs receive and process all initial enquiries: they undertake initial assessments, and provide advice, information, redirection, or 'simple/limited' services as appropriate. 'Simple/limited' services are those services that meet relatively straightforward needs, ranging from registrations and car badges to home care services. The CSTs are also responsible for monitoring and reviewing the home care services they put in place. They refer more complex cases to the Specialist Teams for a full assessment of need.

The Specialist Teams are thus responsible for all cases not dealt with fully by the CSTs. They deal with people whose needs are classified as 'specialist/multiple' or 'complex/comprehensive' and who are therefore deemed to require the services of a care manager. The Specialist Teams are responsible for the full assessment and care management process for such cases and are thus, essentially, care management teams.

Study findings

Mapping the service system

The initial fieldwork attempted to map the Project and mainstream assessment and care management arrangements at system level. This was a research task in its own right and also a necessary precursor to the selection of representative cases for detailed analysis at the individual level. However, the proposed mapping exercise faced a number of problems with information systems. Although difficulties existed in both the Project and the mainstream systems, they were more pronounced in the latter: in neither case was it possible to acquire the requisite data to map the service system as planned. It was decided, therefore, that the study should concentrate on an analysis of detailed case studies charting individuals' pathways through the Project and the mainstream systems respectively (see below).

During this initial fieldwork it became increasingly evident that the function of the mainstream Customer Service Teams needed to be clarified in view of their crucial role in receiving and processing all initial enquiries (see also Dunn, Nicholson, Revely, Simpson and Temple 1994, Newby and Prudhoe 1993). Interviews were conducted with 11 members of the CSTs and Specialist Teams in Darlington and Spennymoor together with four other personnel working closely with these teams. Interviewees referred to difficulties in understanding not only key tasks and processes but the remit of the CSTs; and whilst most interviewees argued that the CSTs concentrated on 'simple/limited' assessments and services, some were concerned that the teams were not taking a holistic, needs-led view of assessment but, rather, were assessing for specific services such as home care.

The importance of appropriate initial assessment and processing of cases was emphasised repeatedly (see also Department of Health 1994a). Project care managers stressed the importance of full assessments in most cases, even where individuals were asking only for a simple service, because apparently straightforward presenting problems often concealed a 'can of worms' in terms of wider and/or more complex needs. The CSTs generally conducted relatively limited assessments and specified limited services; there was concern elsewhere that without a thorough assessment of need the Teams could not know the appropriateness of such services. This concern was echoed in a Project Progress Report, which emphasised that Project care managers 'have consistently urged caution in the concept of simple assessment as defined within a prescribed list of circumstances' (JCP 1994, p.15).

By contrast, however, some staff outside the Project argued that Project care managers spent too much time working on cases that would normally come within the remit of the CST; in other words, simple/limited cases. From the Spennymoor CST's perspective it was said that the team did concentrate on 'initial assessments', some of which are 'simple/limited', but many of which were fairly complex and comprehensive, with assessors 'digging deeper' – similar to care managers from a Specialist Team or the Project.

In Darlington there was some concern about how, after initial assessments, decisions on the most appropriate response were reached. Members of the Darlington CST were worried about the balance between the cases dealt with by the CST itself and those referred to the Specialist Teams.It was argued that the definition of simple/limited assessments – and, therefore, the scope of the CST's responsibility for assessment and subsequent monitoring and review – was too wide. CST members not only felt over-burdened with monitoring and review work, but argued that they were undertaking specialist work that should properly be the responsibility of Specialist Teams. The CST had, it was said, insufficiently experienced staff for this specialist work and could all too easily become a 'dumping ground'.

In Spennymoor, the CST was said to be occasionally frustrated by having to pass on an incomplete case to the Specialist Team and thus not being able to 'see it through'. As a result, the CST had become more flexible in sometimes keeping a case for longer. The Specialist Team, on the other hand, emphasised that the CST enquiry/screening process could take too long: for example, a case taking ten days to be passed on to the Specialist Team. While there was a fast-track system for emergencies, it was argued that delays could lead to emergencies developing unnecessarily.

In examining the broader assessment and care management processes in the Project and mainstream systems, interviewees highlighted difficulties and problems with the latter and were much more positive about the arrangements developed by the Project. In essence, the Project is a Specialist Team that also performs CST functions. Not surprisingly, one of the main advantages of the Project as compared with the mainstream system was that it was responsible for all stages of the assessment and care management process and therefore did not have to contend with problems of clarifying roles and responsibilities between separate teams. A related advantage was that the Project was better able to adopt a detailed and thorough approach to assessment and care management across all of its cases and at all stages of the process. This raises questions about the appropriateness of a screening process provided by two teams rather than a single team.

Individual case studies

The aim of the individual case studies was not only to compare and contrast individual pathways through the Project and mainstream systems but to ascertain users' and other participants' perceptions of, and satisfaction with, the process. Twelve individual cases were selected on the basis of the following criteria:

- person aged 75 or over
- case complexity, i.e. case involving complex needs and requiring some kind of care package
- organisational complexity, i.e. multi-disciplinary in terms of a range of agencies involved
- at monitoring stage (i.e. care package in place).

For each of the Project and mainstream systems in each of the three geographical areas two cases were selected: a 'best case' and an 'average case', which could be either ongoing or closed. The cases, and the relevant interviewees, were selected by care managers: 'best case' was one that best *demonstrated* the system in operation, especially in terms of a user's pathway through the system; 'average case' was one that best *typified* the system in operation, in these same terms. Relevant case files were examined and interviews were conducted by the researchers with six users, seven family members or close friends, and a wide range of professionals from social services, health, and independent sector organisations.

It is worth noting that although this study comprises only a small number of cases it does nevertheless provide an early indication of the operation of the new arrangements based on systematic data collection and analysis. The case studies were designed to address the following questions:

(a) Assessment and care packaging process

- To what extent did assessments take place, and to what extent were they needs-led rather than service-led and holistic rather than partial?

- With regard to hospital discharge, to what extent did needs-led and holistic assessments take place prior to discharge, and to what extent did these provide a solid foundation for the construction of community care packages?

- To what extent did assessments involve input from an appropriate range of professionals on a multi-disciplinary and multi-agency basis?

- To what extent was there a quick response in terms of the progression of the case from enquiry/referral, through assessment, to the provision of a care package?

(b) Care packages and their implementation

- To what extent were care packages based on a thorough exploration of a range of service options, in terms of both service type and sector?

- How systematic were the arrangements for both monitoring and reviewing individual care packages in relation to changing needs?

Findings

(a) The assessment and care packaging process

NEEDS-LED AND HOLISTIC ASSESSMENTS

We explored the extent to which assessments in the Project and the mainstream systems appeared to comprise comprehensive, needs-led, holistic approaches, thus providing sound bases for the design of care packages. There was evidence of a comprehensive assessment providing a sound basis for care package design in each of the six Project cases. By contrast, this was true in only two of the mainstream cases. In the other four mainstream cases there were examples of services being provided before need had been assessed, although there was a subsequent reassessment in three of these cases.

LOCATION OF ASSESSMENT: THE HOSPITAL DISCHARGE DIMENSION

The lack of an holistic approach to assessment – or of any pre-discharge assessment – was apparent in a significant proportion of cases involving discharge from hospital in the mainstream system. More generally, there were concerns about discharge appearing to have been poorly managed. Although one of the mainstream cases provided a particularly good example of a well-planned discharge based on assessed need, even in this instance the user reported that she felt pressurised by hospital staff who repeatedly told her that they needed her bed.

TIMELINESS OF ASSESSMENT

A timely response in terms of assessment and care packaging will maximise the opportunity for prevention and early intervention: this is something which the Project, in particular, always sought to achieve (JCP 1994). In the mainstream system there were four examples of assessments being too late or too slow and one of an assessment being non-existent. By contrast in all six Project cases there was evidence of an holistic assessment providing a sound basis for care packaging; and, furthermore, a quick response in terms of case progression in five of these cases.

JOINTNESS OF ASSESSMENT

As all of the users in these case studies had both health and social care needs, we might have expected the assessments to include input from health personnel; and given the position of the Project Care Managers in an extended primary care team we might have expected this to be more marked there than in the mainstream, simply by virtue of their proximate working relationships. However, the extent of the health input to assessment, as opposed to input to care packages, appeared to be limited to one case in each of the Project and mainstream systems. This is despite the fact that most enquiries and referrals came from health sources: this was the case in five Project cases and four mainstream cases.

The picture with regard to GPs was broadly similar. Although they provided the enquiry/referral in three Project cases and two mainstream cases, there was no evidence of GPs contributing to formal assessments in these or other cases, with the exception of one Project case where the GP reassessed medical needs at the request of the Care Manager.

SPEED OF RESPONSE

Given the fact that Project Care Managers were working closely along-side colleagues in an extended primary care team, we would expect greater speed of response there than in the mainstream. There was considerable evidence that this was indeed the case. Five of the Project cases included examples of a very quick response in terms of the progression from enquiry/referral to care package. By contrast, while four of the mainstream cases showed evidence of a speedy response, it generally related to only one stage of the assessment and care management process, such as conducting a home visit. Moreover, the most striking example of slow response times was in one of the mainstream cases. Two Project cases provided the best examples of quick responses. In the first, the enquiry was followed by an assessment after two days and implementation of the care package by the third. When, a few months later, the district nurse became concerned about a deterioration in the user's health she was able to meet the care manager immediately, and the following day undertake a joint home visit and agree an emergency care plan. The care manager and district nurse attributed their ability to respond quickly (and jointly) to being located in the same building and, specifically, to a good existing relationship, regular personal contact, and accessibility. In the second example, the initial enquiry was followed by an assessment and subsequent admission to a nursing home the same day – the only alternative being (re)admission to hospital. What took half a day in this case would normally, it was said, take three or four days. Such speed was attributed to the following characteristics of Project care managers:

- being part of the practice team
- having established relationships with practice team members (especially the GPs) and with users
- understanding that 'urgent' means urgent
- being a single and clear point of contact
- being immediately and directly available
- adopting a holistic approach
- having a 'personal touch'.

All of these factors were said to be in marked contrast to the situation in the mainstream system.

(b) Care packages and their implementation

COMPONENTS OF CARE PACKAGES AND PROJECT EXPENDITURE

Care packages should be based upon a needs-led, holistic assessment, followed by an exploration of a range of service options. In our case studies, care packages were explicitly underpinned by a comprehensive assessment in each of the six Project cases but only two of the mainstream cases. There was little evidence, across both the Project and mainstream cases, of any exploration of a wide range of non-standard service options. However, one of the Project cases provided an excellent example not only of a range of options being explored but a detailed assessment providing a sound basis for a care plan which was implemented to the satisfaction of both the user and her family.

Most of the community care packages in both the Project and mainstream cases involved home care services, supplemented mainly by day care, respite care, and district nurse visits. There were good examples in both systems of care managers doing everything possible to encourage and enable users to live at home. From our small number of case studies, there did not appear to be evidence of the Project budget having purchased significant elements of these care packages: however, it was used, as intended, to secure a range of additional services for Project clients. In all, 23 per cent of the total Project expenditure of £490,000 was spent on care provision; and of this £111,000 the main elements were, 54 per cent (£60,000) spent on adaptations and 25 per cent (£28,000) on welfare rights. The latter referred to an initiative with the Durham County Council Welfare Rights Unit whereby a specialist full-time Welfare Rights officer and a half-time clerk were appointed to the Project – covering all three practices – from June 1994 to 31st March 1995.

ARRANGEMENTS FOR MONITORING AND REVIEWING CARE PACKAGES

Monitoring and review is an essential part of any dynamic assessment and care management process, but traditionally has been given a lower priority than assessment and care planning (see Department of Health 1994a). There was regular monitoring and review in all six Project cases, with some good examples, as indicated above, of care managers learning about changes in need at a relatively early stage and responding quickly.

There was less emphasis on monitoring and review in our mainstream case studies: it had been undertaken regularly in only three cases. Furthermore, mainstream care managers seemed to learn about changes in need at a relatively later stage and were unable, therefore, to respond in as timely and speedy a fashion as the Project. Also, the comparative lack of a holistic approach to assessment in the main-stream system meant that monitoring and review appeared to be built on less secure foundations than in the Project.

Summary

It is important to stress that the community care reforms are still bedding down and that our findings could therefore be seen as indica-tive of perceived advantages and disadvantages at a very early stage of systems development. The overall finding of this series of case studies was, nevertheless, that the balance of comparative advantage identified in the earlier systems mapping was confirmed. Moreover, this confirmation came from service users and carers as well as from professionals. There was clear evidence, therefore, of the Project being able to operate to the advantage of users in ways not open to the mainstream system. The main reason was that the Project was respon-sible for all stages of the assessment and care management process and therefore did not have to contend with problems of clarifying roles and responsibilities between Customer Services Teams and Specialist Teams. A related advantage was that the Project was better able to adopt a detailed and thorough approach to assessment and care man-agement across all of its cases and at all stages of the process. Thus, although the care packages proved to be broadly similar in terms of care components (and, prior to this, in terms of exploration of a range of service options), the Project cases were generally seen to be dealt with more flexibly and more sensitively in responding to individuals' often rapidly changing needs.

At operational level, there appeared to be a general absence of multidisciplinary assessments in both the Project and mainstream systems. One possible explanation, though not one mentioned by the case study interviewees, was that in the Project the proximity of care managers and health service professionals, by virtue of co-location, meant that assessments were, *de facto*, multidisciplinary. This is likely to be so simply because health professionals referring cases made assessments at the point of referral and conveyed this, however infor-mally, to the co-located care manager. By contrast, care managers in the mainstream system lacked such physical proximity to health service professionals and, thereby, the potential attendant benefits of such informal multidisciplinary working throughout the assessment and care management process.

Conclusion

Our study showed the co-location model to be extremely popular with all concerned and underlined the factors which maximise the chances of securing the goodwill and active co-operation of GPs. The study confirmed that the single most important factor for GPs is having one Social Services contact who works with them consistently and who is able to provide not only easy access and referral but a quick response which, in GPs' terms, 'delivers the goods' of a swift, professional response as needs arise. The Durham Project performed well in precisely these respects and as a result eroded much of what has been a traditional professional stereotyping and mutual suspicion; while at the same time confounding what has long been the conventional wisdom – that projects involving joint working between Social Services and GPs are invariably undermined by issues of parity of legitimacy.

The study showed that, all other things being equal, active co-operation is positively correlated with the proximity and consistency of contact between care managers and GPs and primary health care teams. Full time co-location was seen to be the optimal model in that it maximised the degree of proximity and consistency of contact. Other models may therefore be seen as sub-optimal. They include: care managers co-located but not full-time; Attachment models in which care managers are either full-time but dedicated to more than one practice or are peripatetic; and merely information sharing. It is interesting to note too that there was some anecdotal evidence that the Willington arrangements worked less satisfactorily than the other two Project practices and that one of the main reasons was that the Project Care Manager was only part-time. Undoubtedly, however, another factor contributing to the success of care manager co-location is the existence of a primary health care team that is already operating in an integrated, multidisciplinary way: this was clearly the case in both the Spennymoor and Darlington practices.

In summary, the study showed clearly the advantages that flow directly from the co-location of social services care managers and primary health care professionals in terms of the operation of assessment and care management processes and the consequent fitness, timeliness, and responsiveness of services to individual users' changing needs.

References

Birmingham FHSA (1992) *Community Care Advisers Project – First Stage Evaluation (September 1991 to March 1992)*. Letter from Alan Torbet, General Manager, Birmingham FHSA. Birmingham: Birmingham FHSA.

Bowns, I., Challis, D. and Tong, M. S. (1991) 'Case finding in elderly people: validation of a postal questionnaire.' *British Journal of General Practice 41*, 100–104.

British Medical Association (1992) *Priorities for Community Care. A BMA Report*. April. London: BMA.

Department of Health (1990) *Community Care in the Next Decade and Beyond: Policy Guidance*. London: HMSO.

Department of Health (1994) *Implementing Caring for People: The Role of the GP and Primary Healthcare Team*. London: DoH.

Department of Health (1994a) *Implementing Caring for People: Care Management*. London: DoH.

Dunn, C., Nicholson, S., Revely, N., Simpson, N. and Temple, C. (1994) *Customer Services Team: Definition, Role and Function*. Draft discussion paper. Chester-le-Street, Durham SSD, North Durham Area.

Grace, J. (1992) 'Community care and the GP.' *Geriatric Medicine*, April, 56–59.

Hoddinott, D., Fordham, D., Rodrigues, L. and Royston, S. (1992) *Linking Assessment, Care Management, Commissioning*. Workshop 8 at 'Commissioning for Community Care' Conference, London, 10 July 1992.

House Of Commons Health Committee, Session 1992–93 (1993) *Sixth Report. Community Care: The Way Forward. Volume 1: Report, together with the Proceedings of the Committee. Volume 2: Minutes of Evidence and Appendices*. London: HMSO.

Hudson, B. (1994) 'Breaks in the chain.' *Health Service Journal*, 21 April, 24–26.

Ivory, M. (1993) 'Can the rift be healed?' *Community Care*, 1 April, 6–7.

Ivory, M. (1993a) 'G.P.'s assessment malaise.' *Community Care*, 14 Jan, 6.

JCP (1994) *Joint Commissioning Project. Progress Report: December 1993 to September 1994*. Spennymoor: Joint Commissioning Project.

Kitt, I. (1992) *Proposal for a Joint Commissioning Project in South West Durham and Darlington*. Durham: Durham SSD.

Leedham, I. and Wistow, G. (1993) 'General practitioners and community care.' *Yorkshire Medicine*, Spring 1993, 5, 2, 10–11.

Leedham, I. and Wistow, G. (1993a) 'Key Task 4 – working with GPs.' Community Care, 11.2.93, 17.

Martin, D. (1990) 'Getting it together.' *Health Service Journal*, 28 June, 964–965.

Millar, B. (1993) 'Ignorance is bliss.' *Health Service Journal*, 14 Jan., 12–13.

Newby, K. and Prudhoe, A. (1993) *Evaluation of the Durham Customer Services Pilot Project* (April 1993). Durham: Durham SSD.

Nocon, A. (1993) 'Fair assessment.' *Health Service Journal*, 1 July, 28–29.

Nocon, A. (1992) 'G.P.s' assessments of people aged 75 and over.' Rotherham: Rotherham FHSA.

Royston, S. and Rodrigues, L. (1993) 'Integrated assessment in East Sussex.' *Community Care Management and Planning 1*, 2 June, 35–43.

Secretaries of State For Health, Social Security, Wales and Scotland (1989) *Caring for People. Community Care in the Next Decade and Beyond*. London: HMSO.

Shackley, P. and Donald, S. (1993) 'Prevention in primary care: the annual assessment of elderly people.' *Health Policy 25*, 51–62.

Sparkes, T., Caldicott, H. and Wallace, P. (1993) 'Link working: a consolidated approach to GP based screening of elderly people.' *Scottish Medicine 13*, 1, 5–6.

Torbet, A. (1990) 'Assessment and case management: issues for family health services in the Draft Circular.' In I. Allen (ed) (1990) *Assessment and Case Management*. London: Policy Studies Institute, for the Department of Health.

Chapter 11

Developing Skills in Care Management
A Slow Process

Alison Petch

The implementation of care management must be the example, par excellence, of the gap between the promotion of a concept on paper and the emergence of practice at the front-line. Differences in definitional models, in terminology (case or care management), and in job titles (no less than 23 are listed in JICC, 1993) vie with the scarcity of definitive examples of empirical practice to create a lack of clarity which might suggest that the enthusiasm for the concept has been misplaced. This chapter, in exploring factors which conspire to inhibit more rapid progress, will examine why such action may be premature. It will draw liberally upon a major research programme exploring the implementation of care management in Scotland (Stalker, Taylor and Petch 1994, MacDonald and Myers 1995). Quotations not otherwise referenced are from practitioners interviewed in the course of this study.

Much of the initial enthusiasm for care management in this country derived from the apparent success demonstrated for the approach in the Personal Social Services Research Unit (PSSRU) demonstration projects in Kent (Challis and Davies 1986), Darlington (Challis *et al.* 1995) and Gateshead (Challis *et al.* 1990). Challis (1991) has summarised the key prerequisites of the care manager's function:

- clear and continuing case responsibility
- targeted caseload: older people on the margin of institutional care
- smaller caseloads
- trained and experienced fieldworkers
- decentralised budget, with clear expenditure limits

- knowledge of unit costs of services
- service packages costed
- systematic records for assessment and monitoring
- close health care linkages, either formal or informal.

Likewise, the PSSRU evaluation of the 28 Care in the Community projects (Knapp *et al.* 1992) endorses the benefits of better targeting and of greater autonomy in decision-making, policy formulation and budgetary control.

With a commitment to good case management the cornerstone of high quality care in the White Paper, *Caring for People*, and subsequent detailed guidance for both managers and practitioners (DoH SSI/SWSG 1991a,b), the translation of care management to a much broader canvas might be considered relatively unproblematic. Such an assumption fails to recognise the very different environment of routine practice as compared to the demonstration project, often favoured by additional resources in both cash and kind, and by the spin-offs which accrue from the spotlight of evaluation. The challenges being faced as care management is translated in the more mundane locations of everyday practice will be explored in relation to a number of key dimensions.

Locality needs

An essential backcloth to adequate care management at the individual level is some knowledge of the demography and needs of older people within the local area. Although data for older people may be more accessible than for other care groups, community care plans still wrestle to respond adequately to the challenges of locality-based needs assessment. In the absence of detailed sources on local epidemiology, authorities resort to global incidence figures which may approximate only crudely to the local situation (Stalker 1994a). And yet in many areas there is a ready resource waiting to be tapped for planning purposes in the form of figures held by general practitioners on numbers of older people within their practice. Increasingly, particularly with the development of fund-holders and their own interests in figures for purchasing strategies, more sophisticated data relating to specific needs should also be available.

Clarity of role

The need for care management to be responsive to local factors suggests a requirement for flexibility. Such flexibility, however, vies with a desire for clarity in the appropriate response. The official guidance (DoH SSI/SWSG 1991a) presents a potentially confusing array of at least ten different models of care management, some single agency, others operating on a multi-agency basis in a range of possible configurations. Indeed, it is acknowledged that:

> 'research is not yet able to give definitive guidance on appropriate models, so a period of experimentation is to be encouraged.' (Section 3, para.47)

Evidence from implementation within Scotland suggests that intentions conform to one of three models, the essential distinction being whether care management is perceived as a distinct role with dedicated staffing ('role model') or whether it is intended as a task to be performed by workers alongside other tasks ('task model'). This second model is the most common, with a variant embracing health and social work producing a third model (Stalker 1994b). While valid at the broad structural level, such models may conceal much variation, both inter and intra authority. Available evidence (JICC 1993, DoH SSI 1994) suggests that the characteristic common across the implementation of care management is its diversity – 'as many variations in the models of care management as there are social services departments' (JICC 1993,p.7). Of importance, however, is whether such diversity results from confusion and uncertainty or from considered intent.

As prefaced above, there can also be very different perceptions held by those at different levels within the management hierarchy. Our own work has included interviews with 65 care managers from four regions in Scotland, the two which had adopted the 'role model' and two which were illustrative of a 'task' division. Regions adopting the 'task' model had deliberately avoided the term care management in favour of care co-ordination; in practice there were numerous working definitions of the term in use. Moreover, whatever the new task be called, workers were uncertain as to whether it was different from what they had been doing previously. In contrast, respondents from 'role model' regions would present a familiar list of the seven stages of care management, although, as will be illustrated below, there could be substantial variation in how the stages were handled.

Few care managers felt they had been consulted over the strategies to be adopted within their particular areas. Where consultation did occur it could be dismissed as tokenist.

> 'Prior training should have been two-way…I feel very strongly it was a one-way street.'

Of particular significance is the clarity with which those who are to receive care management have been identified. In the months prior to implementation, much time and many trees were expended in the search for the definitive assessment form. Yet the eligibility criteria determining who should progress to care management were often not made explicit (Petch *et al.* 1994). There is a particular likelihood that where care management tasks are combined with others the threshold for entry to the process remains ill defined, with those involved in the process uncertain as to the nature of their care management workload. There must be an onus on authorities to clarify their criteria. At the planning level, policies, needs and resources must be reconciled, with interventions clearly targeted, while staff require clear guidelines within which to operate. Not least, however, must be the right of the public to know what to expect.

Training

It can be tempting to cite inadequacies in training strategies as an explanation for the slow take-up of innovation. Certainly in Scotland, (MacDonald and Myers 1995) regions in the main appear to have failed to deliver anything substantial in preparation for care management, with the emphasis, if at all, on the mechanics of the assessment process.

> 'No training in care management, though…we had several days training on form filling.'

One of the 'role' regions was the exception in that individuals recruited to take up designated posts from April 1993 received extended training over the previous 12 months, culminating in a five day course. In contrast, one of the 'task' regions was only offering detailed training in May 1995 and encountering difficulties with the disparate audience. Training can be particularly problematic if it is attempted when agendas and responsibilities are still evolving, a scenario found by both Hoyes *et al.* (1994) reporting the experiences of care managers in four English authorities and in our own research:

'We needed training in what the procedures were. We didn't get that because people didn't know what the procedures were. People were making it up as they went along, that's what it felt like.'

It is important, however, not to formulate too simplistic a relationship between training and the introduction of change. Sensitive response to individual needs derives not so much from learning to recite the rhetoric of the latest policy guidance but from transforming one's own practice to listen carefully and respond imaginatively. It is vital that the enormity of the shift from service allocation to needs-based response is recognised. MacDonald and Myers (1995) identify four types of constraints on creativity: external, particularly resource gaps, organisational, cultural and personal. The last two in particular emphasise the need for the flowering of a learning organisation in which service users and those required to respond at all levels strive to work through a continuous learning process.

'It's a two-way process with the person identifying their needs, trying to distinguish needs from wants. It's been a big adjustment – I'm going out with an open mind.'

Thus, rather than delineating the essential components of the care management process through didactic training, its essential form emerges through the process of implementation – 'nothing blocks creativity, it's just starting to think along these lines'. For many, however, the current perception is that they feel so inundated with new procedures and associated administrative demands that innovation and creativity must wait. Limited budgets, discussed in greater detail below, are also perceived as inhibiting. Often overlooked, however, is the fact that the traditional structures of both social and health care professionals tend to conspire against creativity and imaginative thinking. Hierarchical structures are strong, with firm lines of accountability and patterns of regular supervision. Any tendency to initiative tends to be constrained within the security of approved procedures. Such a context leaves a long legacy.

Care manager identity
Particular demands for training can depend upon the background from which care managers have come. Thus, practitioners within generic community care teams identify areas, for example dementia and men-

tal health, where they feel disadvantaged through a lack of previous experience.

> 'The only aspect that concerns me is the legal basis for deciding whether or not people are capable of signing documents for themselves or require a third party. I have asked for training in identifying dementia and when to make this decision.'

Of more long-term importance, however, must be the identity of those who will operate as care managers. Currently, those exercising care management functions are overwhelmingly located within local authority social work or social service departments. Moreover, they exhibit a fairly narrow range of professional backgrounds, predominantly social work with a scattering of occupational therapists. Attitudes to those from within home care can be ambivalent. Despite evidence that agencies are willing to consider a much broader spread (Stalker *et al.* 1994), organisational boundaries are yet to be routinely transcended. Yet there are many situations in which a care manager from the health or voluntary sector would be entirely appropriate. The advantages are most readily evident in relation to those older people with a mental health problem where involvement of a community psychiatric nurse as a care manager may be indicated. For many older people, however, community nursing provision and the management of the interface between hospital and community around discharge procedures is a major focus of activity. For individuals with dementia, a care manager from the voluntary sector may be indicated due to the levels of expertise within the specialist agency. The enduring role of the general practitioner with this care group must also be acknowledged, together with the somewhat uneasy dialogue between care management and the GP (Harris and Porter 1995).

Such proposals, however, encounter all the familiar battles of multiagency working. This can be particularly evident at the assessment stage where, as exemplified by the SSI (1994), there may be reluctance to accept assessments undertaken, for example, by district nurses or health based occupational therapists. Indeed, there is evidence within the single agency of continued duplication at the assessment stage, home care or occupational therapy initiating their own procedure despite completion of the so-called comprehensive assessment. The SSI do report, however, the recognition in one area of social workers from a voluntary organisation as 'accredited assessors' for older people.

Enormous problems remain to be resolved, however, at the boundaries of the different professional inputs across the care management process. Those at the health/social care interface will be most starkly brought to the fore as the impact of the new *Guidance on Access to NHS Continuing Care* begins to be felt. The need for collaboration in this arena may impact more widely on working between the two sectors. Currently, it is not unusual for an older person to be in receipt of home care services as well as of substantial community health care provision, but to completely evade the care management network. Only when a more comprehensive assessment is sought will the potential benefits of care planning be accessed.

Access to budgets

Challis and Davies argued in relation to the early models of care management over ten years ago that:

> 'achieving a new balance between autonomy and accountability might permit a more effective deployment of resources to meet needs.' (1986,p.8)

The most visible evidence of autonomy is the delegation of budgets to the individual care manager, premised from the early pilots as a prerequisite. In certain instances, service users may be their own care managers and thus have access to purchasing their own care. More often the budget is held by the care manager to purchase care on the user's behalf. Some restrictions may be imposed by the local authority in terms of which providers can be used and on the role of the independent sector. Only one of the regions in the Scottish study of implementation had devolved the purchasing role to the care manager, and even in this case the actual budget was held by the senior, the care managers operating with shadow costs and notional limits. Nonetheless, this devolution over purchasing was accompanied by greater autonomy in other aspects of the care planning process, including negotiating individual service contracts for specific clients and arguing for particular local resource development.

In other regions there could be access to ear-marked monies for non-standard provision. Awareness of such allocations varied, however; moreover, the bureaucracy of access could be defeating, not least if it generated delay. Equally disruptive can be the creation of flexibility budgets which are then raided for routine purposes when mainstream budgets are overspent. In one of the regions under scrutiny, non-standard responses had been seriously inhibited by the requirement that all providers were on a standard contracting list. Such a list reinforced the status quo, discriminating against the provider without an established track record with the authority. Implementation of effective care management requires an environment free from unnecessary constraints and rituals.

Care planning

Much of the commentary on the implementation of the new arrangements has focused on the assessment phase (Caldock 1994, Hughes 1993). Yet the strength of the care management process lies in the potential for the long-term co-ordination and adjustment of the response to needs, with a recognition that through the review process assessments are never static. Again, however, there are factors which slow the development of the ideal. The power of the devolved budget has been argued above. An essential accompaniment, however, is access through simple but effective information systems to detailed unit cost information and resource availability. To expect innovative response to need when the care manager has neither the clarity of a purchasing budget or the catalyst of an ingredient list is to apply unnecessary shackles. The inability of social work authorities to activate effective Information Technology (IT) systems both for local use and to communicate across geographical and agency boundaries would suggest that systems need to be externally imposed.

A myriad of uncertainties and practical considerations can further constrain the care manager in their planning task. Practitioners express uncertainty as to the parameters within which they are working and therefore err on the side of caution, unwilling to risk contravention of real or imagined boundaries. Attempts to be more innovative which encounter barriers are likely to act as a disincentive out of proportion to the particular case. Meethan *et al.* (1993) quote the case in the Scarcroft project of the supply of a chair which was found to contravene fire regulations. Abortive efforts of this type we found may discourage, the care manager reverting to the familiar and acceptable response:

'If you take a more imaginative approach, how do you build in safeguards, how can you be sure you're going to get value for money?'

A particular area of uncertainty amongst care managers in our own study was the extent to which they could or should use the independent and particularly the private sector, the specified expenditure requirements of England not being in place. Alternatively, there could be concerns about the accountability of the unfamiliar or the reliability of the informal.

'The care manager just has to jog along, hoping that it's going to work and that she doesn't have the problem of the person not turning up or of exploitation – very anxiety-provoking.'

Care managers may also find themselves frustrated by what they see as the inflexibility of providers: minimum periods of domiciliary care, rigidity at health/social care boundaries, restrictions on the transport of service users in private cars.

'Partly what stops me is the resistance from other agencies against anything which isn't traditional support.'

More general eligibility criteria may also constrain the resources which can be accessed, for example the regulations of Urban Aid funding or the restrictions on the payment of private individuals. Confidence and assertion are necessary for an optimum response to needs, a reason why many would like to characterise the role of care management as one of advocacy.

Crucial to the long-term effectiveness of the care management response is the treatment of unmet need. The controversy generated by the infamous Laming letter in England is misplaced. Knowledge of the shortfall in response is a key building block, even if there are constraints to an immediate response. Scotland did not experience the panic in anticipation of the recording of unmet need; practice in different areas, however, has varied. Most heartening is the strategy in one region where the unmet need recorded on the assessment proforma is aggregated at district level by the contracts officer. This individual has access to a budget and is able to respond at least partially in relation to areas of identified need, possibly negotiating variation with existing providers or arranging for resource provision from the team's care management budget.

'We've seen developments appear after we've reported back that these things are needed, which is quite encouraging. So you're not afraid to say that a service isn't available and what can you do about it. As long as you can gather information and put forward a case there's a good chance of it happening. It's good to have links with providers because if you identify a number of people requiring something similar it may make the case for developing the service.'

It has to be acknowledged, however, that the majority of areas are far from such a scenario. Some, working within a positive culture, may continue to record unmet need in the hope that benefits will start to emerge.

'I'm quite happy to record unmet need. If I think that the client needs something and it's not available and if I feel there's nothing to take its place then it goes down as an unmet need rather than trying to patch together a bit of this and a bit of that. And that's why they're trying to get new services started up.'

Others are less convinced.

'There is a form in the pack for "unmet need" and they're all meant to be banked up and sent to national government who will look at requirements for future budgets. I just never do anything with it.'

In England, also, the completion of the circle which would see the aggregation of data on needs fed back into the planning process at the locality level is at an embryonic stage. Strategic planning of this nature has not traditionally been at the forefront of social work thinking, and as with the hierarchical relaxation necessary for creative thinking, new cultures have to be established. Vertical segregation is endemic within social care – users from front-line workers, workers from management, planners from providers. There is an irony, indeed, if a system designed to encourage liberation from the service-led response through the separation of purchaser and provider instead merely adds to the levels of segregation.

Conclusion

It is essential that impatience at the rate of change does not preclude care management as a routine process being given a fair trial. The complexity inherent in the proposed changes was foreseen in the characterisation by the Audit Commission of the cascade of change (1992):

> 'It will be difficult to manage these changes and there will be constant frustrations on the way.' (para 121)

Yet such sentiments can sound like platitudes to those anxious to see the perceived benefits of care management materialise. If the needs of the individual really are to be the catalyst, a mode of implementation that appears not dissimilar to disjointed incrementalism may appear a disservice. Yet there will always be emerging elements in the external environment to which care management will have to respond: local government re-organisation, shifting boundaries between health and social care provision, new financial constraints and opportunities, further challenges for inter-agency and multi-disciplinary working. The models of care management which become established and survive will be those sufficiently robust to maintain their cohesion yet adjust at the margins. The timescale must be measured in years rather than months; we have hardly begun.

References

Audit Commission (1992) *Community Care: Managing the Cascade of Change.* London: HMSO.

Caldock, K. (1994) 'The new assessment: moving towards holism or new roads to fragmentation?' In D. Challis *et al.* (eds) *Community Care: New Agendas and Challenges from the UK and Overseas.* Arena.

Challis, D. (1991) 'The state of the art.' In S. Onyett and P. Cambridge (eds) *Case Management: Issues in Practice.* University of Kent.

Challis, D. and Davies, B. (1986) *Case Management in Community Care.* Aldershot: Gower.

Challis, D., Chessum, R., Chesterman, J., Luckett, R. and Traske, K. (1990) *Case Management in Social and Health Care : The Gateshead Community Care Scheme.* University of Kent: Personal Social Services Research Unit.

Challis, D., Darton, R., Johnson, L., Stone, M. and Traske, K. (1995) *Care Management and Health Care of Older People.* Arena.

DoH SSI/SWSG (1991a) *Care Management and Assessment: Manager's Guide.* London: HMSO.

DoH SSI/SWSG (1991b) *Care Management and Assessment: Practitioner's Guide.* London: HMSO.

DoH SSI (1994) *Inspection of Assessment and Care Management Arrangements in Social Services Departments October 1993–March 1994.* Second Overview Report.

Harris, J. and Porter, M. (1995) *Health Service Referrals for Community Care.* Department of General Practice, University of Edinburgh.

Hoyes, L., Lart, R., Means, R. and Taylor, M. (1994) *Community Care in Transition.* York: Joseph Rowntree Foundation.

Hughes, B. (1993) 'A model for the comprehensive assessment of older people and their carers.' *British Journal of Social Work 23,* 345–364.

JICC (Joint Initiative for Community Care) (1993) *Care Management: Identifying the Training Needs.* Milton Keynes: Joint Initiative for Community Care.

Knapp, M., Cambridge, P., Thomason, C., Beecham, J., Allen, C. and Darton, R. (1992) *Care in the Community: Challenge and Demonstration.* PSSRU/Ashgate.

MacDonald, C. and Myers, F. (1995) *Assessment and Care Management: The Practitioner Speaks.* Community Care in Scotland Discussion Paper Number 5. University of Stirling: Social Work Research Centre.

Meetham, K., Thompson, C. and Parker, G. (1993) *Making it Happen? Care Management in Practice.* University of York: Social Policy Research Unit.

Petch, A., Stalker, K., Taylor, C. and Taylor, J. (1994) *Assessment and Care Management Pilot Projects in Scotland: An Overview.* Community Care in Scotland Discussion Paper Number 3. University of Stirling: Social Work Research Centre.

Stalker, K. (1994a) 'The best laid plans...gang aft agley? Assessing population needs in Scotland.' *Health and Social Care 2,* 1–9.

Stalker, K. (1994b) 'Implementing care management in Scotland: an overview of initial progress.' *Care in Place 1,* 104–119.

Stalker, K., Taylor, J. and Petch, A. (1994) *Implementing Community Care in Scotland: Early Snapshots.* Community Care in Scotland Discussion Paper Number 4. University of Stirling: Social Work Research Centre.

Chapter 12

Specialist Teams – Are They More Effective?

Roger Fuller and Emmanuelle Tulle-Winton

The debate about specialisation in social work is time-honoured and tangled. Following the Seebohm Report there was intensive, recurring and inconclusive debate about the meaning of its recommendation for 'generic teams' and the alleged implications of specialisation by client group, task or role – a debate resting more on argument and assertion than on empirical evidence (Fuller and Petch 1991). Meanwhile, the drift during the 1970s and 1980s towards increasing formal and informal specialisation by client group (Challis and Ferlie 1987) was both reinforced and re-directed by the community care reforms of 1993, which ushered in a range of relatively new functions (care management, purchasing and providing) alongside earlier specialisms among social services and social work teams engaged with services to the main community care groups (Stalker, Taylor and Petch 1993).

That there has been little research on the effectiveness of different ways of organising teams is in one sense surprising, given the profile of the issue and the frequency of reorganisations in social services and social work departments. In another sense, however, it is not. For several reasons this is a problematic area to study. Notably, the complex idiosyncrasies of local departmental structures create difficulties for the generalisation of findings; and the meanings of 'effectiveness' in the context are far from clear.

In addressing the latter question in this chapter, we will first note some of the claims that may be advanced for the capacity of specialist teams to provide a service to older users that is in some sense 'better' than that available from non-specialist teams. We then draw upon the results of an empirical study to throw light on the validity of these claims, and finally discuss the implications of the evidence – which, as we shall see, are far from straightforward – for the future development of services. At the time of writing, patterns of team organisation within the structure of the community care reforms are still evolving. It therefore seems particularly urgent that what evidence exists about the effectiveness of different modes of team organisation should be considered, and we make no apology for presenting the results of a study conducted shortly before the implementation of the changes.

Claims for specialisation

Specialist teams, defined for present purposes as social services or social work teams composed of professionals working exclusively with older people, appear to have certain distinctive characteristics which perhaps are best seen in terms of their added potential for effective work – with perhaps some corresponding dangers. The existence of a staff group which concentrates upon a single client group may not in itself be coterminous with a high level of experience and expertise, since some members may be relatively inexperienced. Such a group is, however, likely to be more able to create a common culture within the team. Because professionals in other agencies need to relate to fewer social work staff, inter-agency working might be expected to proceed more smoothly through known contacts and increased mutual trust. There may therefore be more opportunity within a specialist team to develop and pool specialist knowledge of the different dimensions of ageing, of skills in working with elderly people, of resources available, and of how to access them. Against this, it might be said that the fact of team specialisation will sometimes necessitate coverage of a larger geographical area, and hence militate against a neighbourhood approach or local community accessibility; and that there may be a risk of an overly professionalised (in a rather vaguely postulated pejorative sense) approach to the task.

In what ways might the potential of specialisation be translated into practice with older people? To the extent that it is, what might be the indicators of the effects of specialisation in day-to-day work? The literature is not particularly helpful at this operational level; in embarking on the study and deciding what kinds of data to collect, we based our thinking primarily on discussion with practitioners. Our deliberations concerning the kind of testable claims that might be made for team specialisation were as follows:

- workers in specialist teams enjoy certain advantages in case-finding; they will receive a higher proportion of 'appropriate' referrals from professional referrers

- their assessments and care plans will show awareness of the specific difficulties experienced by older people and of a range of responses

- their work with clients will be characterised by a wider range of techniques or approaches

- they will have more developed patterns of liaison with other professionals

- the services and support they arrange will be both more imaginative and more consonant with the wishes and needs of users and carers.

The study

Our task was to explore whether different ways of organising social work teams had a measurable effect on the assessment of, and delivery of services to, older people. This called for a comparative study, sufficiently large in scale to permit quantitative analysis and to examine team effects which were independent of local variations in departmental structures. We were also keen to examine the claims that might be made for competing organisational modes. Fifteen teams were selected, in Scotland and the North of England, of contrasting organisational types: seven were specialist 'elderly' teams, five were generic teams with a community social work (CSW) orientation, and three were generic teams where individual workers tended to specialise informally by client group. The latter were called 'hybrid teams' for the purposes of the study, and 'elderly' defined as people of pensionable age. All the teams were located in area offices (rather than being based in hospitals or health centres).

The main data-collection instrument was an adapted version of the case-review form (Goldberg and Warburton 1979). Social workers in each team completed anonymised forms at two stages in the life of a case: after initial allocation and assessment (Time 1) and (for those not closed immediately) after six months or at closure, whichever came earlier (Time 2). All allocated referrals of older people were to be included from a given date up to a target figure for each team; the final sample comprised 1232 cases at Time 1 and 728 at Time 2, the difference between these totals reflecting the number of cases closed immediately following initial assessment and a degree of sample attrition, which did not appear to be biased. Information from the forms covered team variables (teamtype, worker status) referral details (e.g. source, request), client circumstances at referral, social work assessment, activities planned and carried out, and outcomes (including services offered and provided, assessed client well-being, and reason for closure). Small subsamples of clients (N=49) and carers (N=26) were also interviewed.

Overall, the landscape of social work with older people presented by the study is probably a fairly familiar one. Some of its main features are as follows:

- women outnumbered men by two to one, with the modal age group being 76 to 80 years
- 60 per cent lived alone, over half of whom had little or no informal carer support
- 30 per cent of referrals were unspecific; of the rest, 30 per cent were for home help or home care, 18 per cent for day care, 17 per cent for long-term residential care
- 16 per cent were deemed to be at immediate risk to physical or mental health
- one quarter of referrals were recommended for immediate closure after assessment, one quarter of cases remained open for six months or more, and the remainder fell in between
- service provision was dominated numerically by home help or home care and aids and adaptations (each received by over a quarter of clients); for the remainder there was a variety of services provided for relatively small proportions of people, with 8 per cent entering long-term residential care.

The main analysis compared these data between the three teamtypes in order to illuminate the central question of whether team organisation appeared to make any differences of the kind hypothesised above. The analysis therefore compares specialist teams with two different types of generic team. There is an important caveat to be noted here. Both types of generic team comprised workers who tended to specialise individually, on an informal basis, by client group. Some 90 per cent of the sample were dealt with by individual workers, two-thirds or more of whose caseload consisted of older people. What is being tested, then, is specifically the effect of specialist team status on social work activities and outcomes – with the potential implication that being a member of a team constitutes a qualitatively different kind of professional setting from that of the lone specialist in a generic team.

Findings

Broadly, there were both similarities and differences between team-types on the variables included in the study. Where there were differences, the analysis tended to show specialist teams and the (self-styled) community social work teams at opposite ends of a spectrum, with the hybrid teams either at an intermediate point or tending to assimilate to one or the other more distinctive type of team. We were to some extent reassured both that differences were found at all, in a difficult area to research, and that where they were found there was a degree of correspondence to the intuitive grouping of the teams in the sample. Whatever the interpretation of differences, there was some variation, at least, which seemed to call for explanation based on teamtype. Against the obvious possibility that differences might be accounted for by different populations in the 15 areas, we are able to say that there were few obvious differences in the overt characteristics (such as age, sex, and availability of informal support) of clients referred and allocated.

Presentation of results follows, in the main, the natural history of a referral. For reasons of space, tables are presented sparingly; full statistical details are available from the authors. Where differences between teamtypes are reported, this is supported by a statistical significance level of <0.05.

At initial referral

As shown in Table 12.1, the specialist teams had fewer family or self-referrals, and correspondingly more from health centres and other predominantly professional sources. They also had a higher proportion of new referrals, as opposed to those concerning people already known to the department. This seemed to reflect a policy towards case closure confirmed by other findings: the CSW teams, in particular, closed cases earlier, in the expectation that they would subsequently be re-referred if necessary. What the data here most clearly confirms is a hypothesis about the distinctive nature of CSW teams: their accessibility to the community shown in a high rate of self-referral, and their inclination to close cases sooner to avoid 'clientisation'.

Table 12.1: Proportions of cases with selected characteristics referred to each teamtype (N=1232)

	specialist	hybrid	CSW	total
self + family referral*	198 (32%)	94 (30%)	180 (59%)	472 (38%)
health centre referral*	203 (33%)	115 (37%)	39 (13%)	357 (29%)
re-referral+	204 (33%)	115 (27%)	215 (70%)	503 (41%)
total	618	309	305	1232

* X^2 (calculated on complete distribution) = 86.38, df=4, p=0.00
+ X^2 (calculated on complete distribution) = 151.87, df=2, p=0.00

Initial assessment

The findings concerning the immediate outcome of the first period of assessment are among the most striking in the study. On a number of measures, the specialist teams produced more elaborate assessments. Working from an 11-item checklist of 'problems' on the research instrument, they identified a wider range of problems, and higher numbers of problems per case (see Table 12.2). They more frequently noted

Table 12.2: Problems identified at assessment: proportions of cases with each problem by teamtype (N=1232)

	specialist	hybrid	CSW	total
physical care	41%	38%	48%	42%
household management	32%	40%	16%	30%
mobility within home	26%	28%	42%	30%
mobility outside home	28%	19%	27%	26%
social isolation	39%	37%	28%	36%
confusion	13%	9%	7%	11%
dementia	8%	4%	7%	7%
emotional difficulties	14%	10%	5%	11%
family relationships	18%	13%	9%	15%
housing	21%	17%	9%	17%
financial	8%	6%	3%	7%
3+ problems per case	43%	36%	32%	39%
total (N)	618	309	305	1232

problems of 'emotional difficulties', 'confusion' and 'family relation-ships'. When we grouped the individual problems into broader categories, they more often identified problems of well-being or material problems, rather than those of daily living. The specialist teams also assessed the needs of carers as greater.

Care planning

The form asked workers to specify not only those problems which they identified but also those they planned to address; as well as asking broadly what type of services or support was to be offered.

The specialist teams were more likely than others to identify a wider range of problems at assessment than they proposed to address, perhaps implying a distinction in their minds between those problems which are amenable to help and those which are not. Problems relatively less likely to be addressed once identified were those of family relationships, emotional difficulties, social isolation, and confusion. It may be, of course, that the non-specialist teams were disinclined to note the existence of problems they were going to be unable to tackle; if so, they would have some difficulties in recording unmet need. In terms of care planning, whereas the CSW workers had a tendency to plan more frequently for domiciliary services and/or case closure, the specialists were more likely to include in their planning the less tangible areas of social work or community support, and in current terminology were envisaging larger and more varied packages of care. This is noteworthy, as problems or needs being addressed were largely similar across teamtypes.

Case activities and services

Thus far, the data drawn upon relates to Time 1, and has yielded a number of relatively clearcut significant differences between teamtypes. At Time 2, based on forms completed six months later and covering the intervening period, the picture becomes more confused and difficult to interpret.

The second form asked workers to record any newly identified problems arising from changes in circumstances and any re-assessment. Perhaps surprisingly, in view of the finding at initial assessment, there were no significant differences between the teams here.

**Table 12.3: Proportion of cases showing high levels
of contact with other professionals (N=726)**

	specialist	hybrid	CSW	total
in own dep't*	174 (42%)	39 (32%)	60 (31%)	273 (38%)
GPs, other H.				
centre+	61 (15%)	9 (7%)	7 (4%)	77 (11%)
total	411	121	194	726

* X^2 (calculated on complete distribution) = 9.09, df=2, p=0.01
+ X^2 (calculated on complete distribution) = 19.08, df=2, p=0.00

Workers were also asked to record their activities as social workers during the life of a case, and their liaison with other agencies. From an eight-item checklist of activities, workers from all teams noted 'arranging services' and 'providing information' most frequently. It appeared that the specialist teams had a more varied repertoire, being (for example) more likely to include 'counselling', 'supporting carers', and 'advocacy'. They also recorded a higher number of different activities per case. Overall, active liaison with other agencies was noted in only a minority of cases, though (again) it was the specialists who were more often sharing information and planning decisions with, for example, health professionals (see Table 12.3). They also reported discussing cases more frequently with other disciplines from their own department, and in supervision.

Data on actual service provision is clearly complicated by variations in local service availability and, perhaps, by underlying local traditions in response (four of the five CSW teams were from the same urban department). There were some significant differences between teamtypes in services both offered and provided. Specialist teams provided significantly more packages with a focus on support outside the home, such as day care and respite or (in a small minority of cases) long-term residential care. This applied particularly to older people (i.e. those aged over 80), regardless of their physical or mental competence. CSW and hybrid teams provided more services within the home. As a general rule, however, younger clients were more likely to receive domiciliary support regardless of teamtype. Such differences are difficult to relate to any plausible hypothesis about the effect of teamtype.

The Time 2 data on case closure produced major differences between teams, confirming the earlier suggestion from Time 1. The CSW teams closed cases sooner (over half being closed within six weeks of allocation) and had fewer cases open at the end of the monitoring period. Unlike the specialist teams, they appeared to be operating a clear 'high throughput' policy.

Outcomes

Apart from service receipt, there were two measures of outcome available in the study: social workers' perceptions at Time 2 of client state, well-being, and the degree to which needs had been met; and interview material from a subsample of clients and carers. In both cases the findings are inconclusive.

There was no tendency for clients of different teams to be assessed as benefiting either more or less from the various kinds of help received. While some problems, such as confusion, were seen as less amenable to help than others, this was true across the whole sample. There was likewise no tendency for clients at interview, selected explicitly to contrast specialist and CSW teams, to express greater or lesser satisfaction with the process of assessment and the response to identified needs. On the whole, those interviewed who reported dissatisfaction did not tend to be from particular areas or teamtypes. They differed from other respondents in personal characteristics, being more confident, often younger, and disabled because of chronic illness.

It must be admitted that both of these measures are less than perfect. The social workers' perceptions, though consistent across the three separate indicators mentioned above, may well reflect the level of social worker sanguinity – there appears to be a remarkable tendency for social workers across many different fields to say they have been successful approximately two-thirds of the time! (Fuller 1992). The client interviews were carried out retrospectively, and there were problems of recall. Although we attempted to go beyond the bland satisfaction questions which usually attract a positive response (Wilson 1993), the range of dissatisfactions revealed did not vary by teamtype. More wide-ranging interviews conducted prospectively, or at least a contact closer to the time and based on the clients' own expectations prior to initial contact, might have elicited differences.

Significance of the findings

The findings so far reported are based on initial analyses testing for simple relationships between teamtype and other variables. We might at this stage conclude that specialist teams, when compared with others, are characterised by a higher rate of referrals from professionals rather than the community, and subsequently a higher degree of contact with other professionals; by a capacity to identify a wider range of problems at assessment; and by a larger and more varied set of activities in face-to-face work with clients and their carers. We have not been able to demonstrate, admittedly through methods which may be more adapted to detecting social work activities than client outcomes, that their clients are better off or more satisfied as a result.

But the data needs to be examined more closely than this. For there were potential factors at work which differed from teamtype, but were associated with it. For example, the CSW teams had a preponderance of re-referred cases, and a preponderance of cases which were open for a relatively short time. In neither instance is it immediately apparent that these features are entailed by a CSW approach; although it is possible to construct an affinity between the high throughput model of social work intervention that they imply and some versions of CSW, it is also perfectly possible for a specialist team to open and close cases quickly in the expectation of a proportion of early re-referrals. It might, however, be that the associations found between teamtype and certain variables are 'really' an association between these variables and case duration or re-referral status. In fact, when relationships between variables are examined, it turns out that there are indeed qualifications to be made to the first-run findings.

First, the distinctiveness of specialist teams at assessment applied more strongly to re-referrals than to new referrals. The most plausible explanation for this would seem to be that where cases were re-referred to CSW teams, soon after a previous involvement, the needs and problems were assumed to be known, and they received less attention than newly referred cases. The specialist team workers, by contrast, appeared to apply a more thoroughgoing assessment consistently across their workload.

Second, the tendency of the specialist teams to have a higher degree of liaison with other agencies applied most particularly in cases of longer duration, which represented a higher proportion of their caseload than that of the CSW teams. It is perhaps a truism that cases which remain open longer provide more opportunity for relationships with other professionals. It is also the case that the longer cases seemed also to be the more 'eventful' ones, with little evidence of cases being kept open in a 'monitoring only' category; this would create a greater need for liaison across and outwith departments.

These qualifications, however, modify but do not run counter to the findings reported earlier. Rather, they point to the likelihood that the effects of team organisation are not unilinear; not surprisingly, they operate in the context of other factors, including the style of social work adopted.

Is specialisation effective?

There is, of course, no one answer to this question. The study has provided some evidence for a team effect, if one that operates in complex interaction with other factors. It does appear that some of the claims made for specialisation can be upheld some of the time. The specialist teams' work was marked by more elaborate and wider-ranging assessment and care planning, and by a richer repertoire of client-related activities; all consistent with a use of specialist knowledge and skill. There was evidence of a more developed relationship between the specialists and other agencies, both at the referral stage and in the context of longer-term casework – if in a minority of cases. What has not been established is a measurably better outcome for clients. There is therefore some support for a rather depressing hypothesis: that the specialists' added awareness at the assessment and planning stage and their deployment of a wider range of skills did not, in the end, make much difference.

This may well be a reflection of the undoubted fact that client outcomes are more difficult to identify and measure than are social work procedures. If, however, there is some truth in the proposition, it would not, perhaps, be altogether surprising. Assessment and planning skills can in themselves make little impact if adequate and suitable resources are not available to implement the plans. Likewise, clear-sightedness in identifying problems is of limited use if the problems themselves are of such an intractable nature that the effect of social work can at best be marginal – which is likely to be the case with a significant proportion of older people. For example, one respondent was in acute and constant pain from rheumatoid arthritis; the support provided by his social worker and his wife dealt with the mobility problems but not the pain. Another had found himself at the centre of a family feud in relation to his current and future care; day care provided some support to his family without resolving the basic conflict over who should take responsibility for care and how differences should be resolved. In this context, it is for debate whether, for example, the tendency of the specialist team workers to identify more problems than they proposed to address is preferable to the tendency of the CSW workers to identify only those problems which they could address and to deliver an immediate response.

One implication of this is to question whether it makes sense to undertake a simple comparison between different ways of organising teams in the hope of determining that one or another is the optimal choice. It may be, quite simply, that there is more than one way of doing effective social work. Quite apart from the competing claims of a generic mode of organisation which, almost by definition, cannot be tested in a study based on a single client group – that, for example, specialists in ageing may be ill-prepared for tackling issues arising in the wider family of the older person – perhaps the real question is one of the fit between organisational type and particular styles of social work. The CSW teams in the study appeared to have developed a distinctive style of working which had a degree of compatibility with their approach; the specialist teams less clearly so.

This having been said, certain issues assumed greater prominence than when the study was conducted, including the higher profile now given to supporting carers and the obligation to record unmet need. To translate the strengths of the specialist teams into the new organisational configurations of the community care reforms is a task that awaits further deliberation from practitioners, managers, and those concerned with social work training. The results of this study, conducted on the eve of the reforms, would point in certain directions, including:

- the advantages of a specialist input at the assessment stage
- the significance of a stable group of knowledgeable workers for promoting inter-agency collaboration
- the continuing importance of retaining the social work skills which the specialists demonstrate

- the greater awareness of the support needs of carers demonstrated by the specialists
- the advantages for recording unmet need of the specialists' tendency, as demonstrated in this study, to identify needs they were unable to address.

References

Challis, D. and Ferlie, E. (1987) 'Changing patterns of fieldwork organisation II: the team leaders' view.' *British Journal of Social Work 16*, 181–202.

Fuller, R. and Petch, A. (1991) 'Does area team organisation make a difference?' *British Journal of Social Work 21*, 471–489.

Fuller, R. (1992) *In Search of Prevention*. Aldershot: Avebury.

Goldberg, E.M. and Warburton, W. (1979) *Ends and Means in Social Work* London: George Allen and Unwin.

Stalker, K., Taylor, J. and Petch, A. (1993) *Implementing Community Care in Scotland*. Community Care in Scotland Discussion Paper No 4. University of Stirling: Social Work Research Centre.

Wilson, G. (1993) 'Users and providers: different perspectives on community care services.' *Journal of Social Policy 22*, 4, 507–526.

Chapter 13

Changing Practice
Professional Attitudes, Consumerism and Empowerment

Olive Stevenson

This final chapter focuses on older people who workers in social service or social work departments may need to help. It is about primary users of services rather than the carers, vital as the latter are in the whole process of social care. There is now a significant body of research and literature on the role of carers. Some of the general issues raised here are applicable both to user and carer; but I believe it is timely to concentrate some attention on the feelings, needs and wishes of those older people who may become service recipients.

The development of social work with older people

Growing professional interest

When the history of British social work comes to be written, the period from the mid-1980s to the end of the 1990s may be seen to have been crucial in consolidating or weakening the position of older people in relation to 'the professionals' and agencies who are supposed to serve them. At the time of writing, it is difficult to predict which way it will go, for there are contradictory signs.

First, the good news: we have moved a long way from the 'taken-for-granted' ageist assumptions of the 1960s and 1970s, mirrored in the findings of our research at the time (Parsloe and Stevenson 1978) on social service teams, where we found, as have others, that very little qualified social work time went into work with older people and that attitudes expressed towards them were frequently patronising, if not derogatory. Social work attitudes have been affected by a burgeoning sociological/gerontological and social policy literature.

There have been well-received books by social workers about older people (Rowlings 1981, Marshall 1983, Stevenson 1989). Feminist interest in older women has increased, if belatedly and rather more in carers than cared for. (See, for example, Lewis and Meredith 1988, Nissel and Bonnerjea 1982).

The 'feminisation of later life', as Arber and Ginn (1991) put it, has encouraged quite a powerful analysis of the 'double jeopardy' of sexism and ageism and of the extent to which older women are placed at a social and economic disadvantage through processes of structured dependency (Walker 1980). Obviously, social workers are not immune from these influences. Most recently, the development of specialisms in the second year of social work courses has offered students the opportunity to address issues concerning old people in greater depth than previously.

A second aspect of good news concerns the well rehearsed ideals of community care policy, with its emphasis on empowerment of service users and on partnership between user and provider. In 1991, one read with something approaching amazement, the assertion in government policy that:

> 'The rationale for this reorganisation is the empowerment of users and carers. Instead of users and carers being subordinate to the wishes of service providers, the roles will be progressively adjusted. In this way, users and carers will be enabled to exercise the same power as consumers of other services.' (SSI/SWSG 1991, Care Management and Practitioners' Guide)

This neatly captured the ideological ground, claimed by the left and right politically. The term 'empowerment' was acceptable to the former; yet the latter used related (though by no means identical) concepts, such as consumerism, with which they felt comfortable. The rather strange alliance produced a rhetoric for community care which social workers could endorse, albeit with doubts and cynicism. As I have argued (Parsloe and Stevenson 1993):

> 'social services department have a benchmark against which to test every aspect of the structure, management and work of the organisation. The central question to be asked is – does it enhance the power of users and carers?...It provides a star to steer by even if at times clouded by inadequate resources and failures of imagination.' (p.9)

Thus, raised awareness of the position (and the predicament) of many older people, especially women, and an assertion of the ideal of empowerment for all users combined to offer a real opportunity to make progress in offering more sensitive and imaginative services than before, in which the feelings and wishes of the older person would be respected.

If that sounds too rosy, it is worth reminding ourselves than in two related areas of concern, work with carers and work with people with a learning disability, we have seen social workers transform their understanding and practice in a relatively short period of time. Paradoxically, the fact that some social workers and students will (rightly) point out how much more needs to be done, confirms the point! Only a few years ago, the issues were simply not alive and the debate did not take place. So why should we not transform practice with older people?

Organisational constraints

There is, regrettably, some bad news which places this in jeopardy. The first and most obvious bad news concerns the shortage of resources. As this chapter is being written, the Association of Directors of Social Services has claimed that at least 80 per cent of their departments are being forced to make cuts; services to older people are high on that agenda. This is not the place to discuss the detailed impact of public expenditure constraints. Its relevance to this discussion is that 'consumerism' is, in the rhetoric of government, linked to 'choice'. Severe resource shortages make a mockery of the ideal of choice in the key process of care management and the assembly of packages of care, or in decisions concerning admission to residential care. More subtly, a counter rhetoric amongst social workers may develop in which everything is blamed on resource shortages. This may have the effect of stifling creative and imaginative activity in planning for and with individuals. It is no exaggeration to say that the next few years will decide the credibility of the policy which offered in theory a real opportunity for the empowerment of older people.

A second difficulty concerns what might be described as the 'procedural preoccupations' of social service and social work departments. More familiar, and much discussed, is the dominance of procedures in child protection work but, in fact, this is but one aspect of an organisational trend which is more pervasive. It is inevitable, and proper, that large welfare agencies develop bureaucratic mechanisms which establish eligibility criteria and accountability, to name but two factors. However, the danger is that these mechanisms become dominant and impair the quality of face-to-face relationships, either because of the time which administrative activity takes or because the mechanisms are used insensitively. A classic example of the latter concerns the design and use of forms. When undertaking the Rowntree research referred to above, we formed the impression that some workers saw 'the forms' as an obstacle to making a sensitive assessment rather than as an aid. Over many years, the mystification and confusion experienced by social security claimants in relation to 'filling in the forms' has been much discussed by social workers. The disempowering effect when claimant meets form is well understood. Their use in community care assessment needs careful appraisal in relation to their impact on users.

A further, more recent, aspect of bureaucratic social services activity concerns the purchaser/provider split. When this is taken down to the level of the individual, as distinct from the provision of services 'en bloc', there must be mechanisms for ensuring that 'the provider' is kept in touch with the impact of services on the recipient. The manner in which services are delivered is a crucial factor in empowering or disempowering the user.

A third element of possible 'bad news' concerns attitudes of managers and workers toward this user group. I referred earlier to anti-ageist movements and their impact on social workers. Yet the advances were tentative, the achievements fragile. Consistent efforts have to be made, but notably in education and training at all stages. The fact that, in volume, old people are overwhelmingly the dominant group requiring support in the community and residential care may have a negative impact. They are not 'special', they are 'run of the mill'. Most important, they may not be seen as interesting people whose needs and feelings require understanding every bit as sophisticated as other adults. Energetic advocacy for other user groups – such as younger people with mental or physical disabilities, although commendable in themselves, throw a spotlight on other community care users whilst very old people are left in the shade. We are still hearing of unqualified workers 'taking on the elderly'; a point to which attention was drawn more than 15 years ago (Parsloe and Stevenson 1978).

Thus, it can be seen that we are on a knife-edge in relation to quality of service to very old people. Will the opportunities afforded by a growth of interest and understanding among academics, especially the gerontologists, and by community care policies which had the seeds within them of sensitive and empowering practice, be grasped? Or will they be lost by a combination of resource scarcity and insensitive bureaucratisation? The remaining part of this chapter develops some key issues which are critical to the implementation of empowering services to old people.

Old people: the same or different?

At the heart of the concept of empowerment lies a moral assumption – that it is desirable to shift the balance of power, in our case, between worker and user. Indeed, the very endorsement of the ideal leads on to the articulation of rights, a process well illustrated at present in the field of disability. However, those on the side of the angels, enthusiasts for empowerment in social work, sometimes lack sophistication in formulating realistic goals and sensitive ways of working which take account of the individual's wishes and preoccupations, of their world view and of the limitations and constraints imposed by their characteristics.

If we wish to empower very old people who are in need of services, we have, simultaneously, to see them both as the same and as different from other adults. They are the same in terms of the value and respect we should accord to them; they have the same needs and problems in relationships. Yet there are certain differences which have important implications for work with them. Some are familiar, though nonetheless important, and spring from the undeniable fact of physiological ageing (Briggs 1990). Of course, as gerontologists are fond of pointing out, ageing begins decades before old age as conventionally defined. There are, however, well known hazards of old age which are related to biological processes. Two of these are falls and inability to keep warm. Falls and their consequences, such as hip fractures, frequently mark a turning point in the lives of old people and sharply increase mortality and dependence. The weakening of the body's 'thermostats' makes it essential for elderly people to live in higher temperatures; the consequences of a cold home go far beyond hypothermia to cold-related morbidity and mortality, shamefully high in the UK. So what has all this to do with empowerment? It suggests that preventive strategies, both at a community and individual level, are a crucial part of effective support. Education and information for older people are of great importance in these strategies, because some of these basic needs for home safety are not well understood (for example, chairs of the right height), nor are the very serious health implications of not being warm enough. Clearly, however, it is a matter not simply of knowledge but of resources, though the cost of many home and domestic improvements is often not high. No social worker with old people at home should neglect 'an audit' of home conditions.

Some realities of life in old age

An uncomfortable fact which has to be faced concerns the incidence of disability, which rises very sharply after age 70 or 75 (OPCS 1989). The rather unattractive phrase which has been coined to describe this period of life is 'compressed morbidity'. While the health of adults has improved beyond recognition during this century, medical science does not yet protect us from serious and multiple-minor disabilities in the last years. It is important to distinguish, if only to combat ageist assumptions, between the processes of ageing *per se* and certain age-related diseases, notably arthritis and dementia, for which at present little can be done. However, so far as the consequences for social work intervention are concerned, the distinction is not significant. Very old people, especially women, face a wide range of debilitating and frustrating conditions, which seriously limit mobility and/or social engagement. The taken-for-granted activities of adult life which create a sense of freedom and choice, integral to empowerment, are denied to many. These difficulties are compounded by the fact that so many old women live alone and are deprived of ordinary opportunities for social stimulation. Thus, a central concern for social workers has to be how best to limit, control and remedy the effects of disability which so often is deeply disempowering.

When we consider cognitive processes in ageing, the evidence and its implications are less clear. Leaving aside the disease dementia, it is not self-evident that ageing necessarily brings cognitive decline. It is all too easy for social workers to elide physical and mental decline. For example, research indicates that old people take longer to learn new things (Coleman 1990) but even that is challenged by the oft-cited Australian research in which very old people learnt a new language,

German, faster than the youngsters! (Naylor and Harwood 1977). Nor is speed necessarily a virtue; it has been suggested that old people take longer to reach a more considered view or decision or see situations in greater complexity (Cohen and Faulkner 1984). This matter poses a particular challenge to social workers because of the great variation in cognitive functioning which is observable in very old people. In face-to-face contact, it is alarmingly easy to appear condescending; yet effective communication may require an adaptation of pace and more time to go over things. Furthermore, faced often with hearing loss and sometimes a lack of stimulation which results in sensory deprivation it is not easy to make an assessment of mental capacity. If an ideal of empowerment requires the practitioner to involve the user in making decisions, communication skills with very old people become paramount. This has been widely acknowledged in relation to people with learning disabilities but is much less developed in the field with which we are concerned. There is much room for detailed and evaluated work. Nor should it be forgotten that some of the decisions which very old people have to take, notably those concerning entry to residential care, are of huge significance. Working through the thoughts and feelings associated with this, going over the issues, may be a lengthy and at times circular process.

Traumatic life events and changes

Even if the decisions to be taken are less fundamental, the need to take them often arises from a traumatic change in life circumstances. This has been admirably illustrated in recent research by Baldock and Ungerson (Baldock and Ungerson 1995). In a study of 32 stroke victims (of whom nearly all were over 60 and a majority over 70) who returned home, they draw attention to the 'unscripted nature of dependency' (p.43); that is to say, most of the people they interviewed 'had few ideas as to what can be done' and... 'more importantly, they were very uncertain as what should be done'... 'This was not simply a cognitive problem to do with knowledge about available provision', (p.44). *'The obstacles to user or consumer understanding of the care system are primarily to do with values and culture rather than matters of fact and information'*, (p.45). Baldock and Ungerson discuss the obstacles to consumer participation; first, emotional distress, involving 'adjustments in routine and consequently self-image, identity and relationships...Almost always these have to do with a decision about organising care', (p.46). Second, the consumer culture and the care market; 'what people are prepared to buy is not a simple function of wants and an ability to pay...Even where people knew of services and products, needed them and could afford them, they still found the prospect of buying them uncomfortable or inappropriate in some way', (p.47). Baldock and Ungerson also point out that there were wide variations among their sample in attitudes to participating in the care market.

Multiple roles for care managers

This excellent study, which should be invaluable to social workers, indicates that there are likely to be very different views among users as to what constitutes 'empowerment' in the arrangement of care services. The study illustrates the interaction of emotional factors with practical arrangements and indicates those who seek to help must have an appropriate mix of skills. Whether intentionally or not, the authors make an overwhelming case for care managers to be more than good administrators. If they are not to be social workers, they must behave like them, (at their best!) (Stevenson 1996). Recently, the Joseph Rowntree Foundation has reported on research (Zarb and Nadash 1994) by the Policy Studies Institute, into direct payment for personal assistance by disabled people and the government has indicated a willingness to develop along these lines. The study finds that 'disabled people using the payments option almost invariably expressed greater satisfaction with the choice and control over their support arrangements and the reliability of provision than did those using services' (Jospeh Rowntree Social Policy Research Findings 64, 1994). Such arrangements were also reported to be cheaper; which no doubt is a factor in ministerial decisions.

No one should deny the importance of this option to some in their wish to control their destinies. However, it is no part of an empowerment ideal to abdicate responsibility for support and protection for those who are not willing or able to manage their lives. At its simplest, some very old people are tired, often as a result of pain. They have made decisions and choices all their lives and would like someone else to take over. Others are depressed. Much more complex are the hundreds of thousands of cases in which the old person has a degree of mental impairment, consequent upon common conditions like dementia or

Parkinson's disease. At the extreme end of these sad illnesses, there is no dilemma about autonomy for such people are not capable of managing their lives. (Even then, there are major issues surrounding their affirmation as people and the ways in which residential care can protect their damaged identity (Kitson 1990). Complex questions arise, concerning, for example, the use of medication or of restraints, including locked doors).

However, for most practising social workers who work with old people in the community, it is those who are less severely impaired who pose the greatest problems if workers are sincerely committed to an empowering ideal. In a process in which decline seems inevitable, the task and the problem which requires sensitive skill, is to preserve the opportunities for choice and decisions wherever possible but to recognise an equivalent moral duty to protect a vulnerable person.

Protecting vulnerable adults

Both the English and Scottish Law Commissions (1995) have severally recently published consultative documents in which legal reform to protect vulnerable adults is strongly recommended. Recognising the dangers of the erosion of autonomy, the English document suggests four criteria of the 'person's best interests' on which decisions concerning vulnerable adults should be taken. These are:

(1) The ascertainable past and present wishes and feelings of the person concerned and the factors that person would consider if they were able to do so.

(2) The need to permit and encourage the person to participate or to improve his or her ability to participate, as fully as possible in anything done for, and any decision affecting him or her.

(3) The views of other people whom it is appropriate and practicable to consult about the person's wishes and feelings and what would be in his or her best interests.

(4) Whether the purpose for which any action or decision is required can be as effectively achieved in a manner less restrictive of the person's freedom of action (p.45).

It is hard to conceive of better guidelines for social workers in their daily practice and infinitely sad that they are often not followed by professionals across agencies.

In asking the question – 'are very old people the same or different from other adults?' I have emphasised differences to counteract the simplistic rhetoric of empowerment which often lacks focus and detail on the specific needs and characteristics of particular user groups. In conclusion, however, let me tip the pendulum in the other direction, to point out that the basic human needs are indeed identical. It is the manner of satisfying these which has to be varied, both in terms of this particular group and of the unique individuals within it. There is one especially important common theme for all adults, which sadly is little discussed in relation to the empowerment of very old people. That is the need to give as well as to receive. The difficulties which have been discussed above often create situations in which the old person feels continually obligated and has little chance of reciprocal activity, in contrast to 'younger' old people who are frequently pivotal in family and community support. The often-heard 'what have I got to live for?' is as much about being useful as it is about activity and enjoyment divorced from relationship. In the instrumental, pressurised world of community care and the care market, can social workers reflect and act on this deep human need, both in the way they offer help and in the way services are developed? (Transport to enable support of an ailing friend or sister, otherwise inaccessible, is but one example).

There is no field of social work in which empowerment is more urgent and requires more skill than with very old people. It is urgent because of the gravity of the service needs of this large and growing sector of our population, attitudes to whom have often been demeaning, condescending and oppressive. The time is ripe for the development of principled skills which acknowledge vulnerability and the need for protection while zealously guarding autonomy.

References

Arber, S. and Ginn, J. (1991) *Gender and Later Life*. London: Sage.

Baldock, J. and Ungerson, C. (1995) *Becoming Consumers of Community Care: Households within the Mixed Economy Welfare*. York: Joseph Rowntree Foundation.

Briggs, R. (1990) 'Biological ageing.' In J. Bond and P. Coleman (eds) *Ageing in Society*. London: Sage.

Cohen, G. and Faulkner, D. (1984) 'Memory in old age "good in parts".' *New Scientist 11*, October, 49–51.

Coleman, P. (1990) 'Psychological ageing.' In J. Bond and P. Coleman (eds) *Ageing in Society*. London, Newbury Park, New Delhi: Sage Publications.

Kitwood, T. (1990) 'The dialectics of dementia:with particular reference to Alzheimer's Disease.' *Ageing and Society 10*, 177–196.

The Law Commission (1995) *Mental Incapacity*. Law Commission No. 231. London: HMSO.

Lewis, J. and Meredith, B. (1988) *Daughters Who Care*. London and New York: Routledge.

Marshall, M. (1983) *Social Work with Old People. Practical Social Work Services*. BASW/MacMillan.

Naylor, G.F.K. and Harwood, E. (1977) 'Das akademische Lerner bei alter Menschen.' *Sn Actuelle Gerontologic 7*, 397–400.

Nissel, M. and Bonnerjea, L. (1982) *Family Care of the Handicapped Elderly. Who Pays?* London: Policy Studies Institute.

Office of Population Censuses and Surveys (1989) *Surveys of Disability*. Report I. London: HMSO.

Parsloe, P. and Stevenson, O. (1978) *Social Service Teams: The Practitioner's View*. London: HMSO.

Parsloe, P. and Stevenson, O. (1993) *Community Care and Empowerment*. York: Joseph Rowntree Foundation.

Rowlings, C. (1981) *Social Work with Elderly People*. London: George Allen and Unwin.

Social Policy Research Findings (1994) *Direct Payments for Personal Assistance, November 1994*. York: Joseph Rowntree Foundation.

SSI/SWSG (1991) *Care Management and Assessment: Practitioners' Guide*. London: HMSO.

Stevenson, O. (1989) *Age and Vulnerability: A Guide to Better Care*. London: Edward Arnold.

Stevenson, O. (forthcoming) 'Care management: does social work have a future?' *Journal of Social Work Education*.

Walker, A. (1980) 'The social creation of poverty and dependency in old age.' *Ageing and Society 1*, 1, 73–94.

Zarb, G. and Nadash, P. (1994) *Cashing in on Independence: Comparing the Costs and Benefits of Cash and Services*. British Council of Organisations of Disabled People, De Bradelei House, Chapel Street, Belper, Derbyshire DE5 1AR.

The Contributors

Rosemary Bland is Lecturer in Social Work, University of Stirling, currently on secondment to the Social Work Services Inspectorate of the Scottish Office.

Julie Curran is Consultant in the Psychiatry of Old Age, Whyteman's Brae Hospital, Kirkcaldy, Fife.

Bridget Franklin is Research Fellow, Centre for Housing Management and Development, University of Wales, Cardiff.

Roger Fuller is Deputy Director of the Social Work Research Centre, University of Stirling.

Brian Hardy is Senior Research Fellow, Community Care Division, Nuffield Institute for Health, University of Leeds.

Enid Levin is Research Fellow, National Institute of Social Work, London.

Ian Leedham is Visiting Fellow, Community Care Division, Nuffield Institute for Health, University of Leeds.

Charlotte MacDonald is Research Fellow, Social Work Research Centre, University of Stirling.

Jo Moriarty is Research Fellow, National Institute of Social Work, London.

Fiona Myers is Research Fellow, Queen Margaret College, Edinburgh.

Gillian Parker is Professor and Director of the Nuffield Community Care Studies Unit, University of Leicester.

Alison Petch is Professor and Director of the Nuffield Centre for Community Care Studies, University of Glasgow.

Chris Phillipson   is Professor of Applied Social Studies and
                                   Social Gerontology, University of Keele.

Olive Stevenson   is Professor of Social Work Studies, University
                                   of Nottingham.

Neil Thompson   is Professor of Social Work, University of
                                   Staffordshire.

Emmanuelle Tulle-Winton   is Lecturer in Sociology, Glasgow Caledonian
                                   University.

Christina Victor   is Senior Lecturer in Health Services Research,
                                   St. George's Hospital Medical School, London.

Alan Walker   is Professor of Social Policy, University of
                                   Sheffield.

Tony Warnes   is Professor of Social Gerontology in the
                                   Faculty of Medicine, University of Sheffield.

Gerard Wistow   is Professor of Health and Social Care,
                                   Nuffield Institute for Health, University of
                                   Leeds.